THE WITNESS OF PEBBLES

THE WITNESS OF PEBBLES

Poems and Portrayals

by

ROGER WHITE

with an introduction by
Geoffrey Nash

GEORGE RONALD
OXFORD

First published by
George Ronald
46 High Street, Kidlington, Oxford OX5 2DN

Acknowledgements

Some of these poems and portrayals have appeared in the following publications:
Bahá'í Studies, vol. 7 (Canadian Association for Studies on the Bahá'í Faith): ed. Dr Peter Morgan
The Bahá'í World, vols. XVI, XVII (Israel): ed. under the supervision of the Universal House of Justice
Canadian Encounter, 1980, 1981 (Canada): ed. Elizabeth St Jacques
Dandelion, No. 2 (United Kingdom): ed. Joaquina D. González-Marina
Glory (National Bahá'í Youth Committee of India): ed. Marzia Rowhani
Gouttelettes (National Spiritual Assmbly of the Bahá'ís of Switzerland): ed Isabelle Aubert
Light of the Pacific (National Spiritual Assembly of the Bahá'ís of the Hawaiian Islands): ed. Elizabeth Hollinger
New Day (National Spiritual Assembly of the Bahá'ís of the Republic of Ireland): ed. Tony McGinley
New Zealand Bahá'í Newsletter (National Spiritual Assembly of the Bahá'ís of New Zealand)
Voices of Israel, vols. 7, 8 (Israel): ed. Reuben Rose
World Citizen (National Bahá'í Youth Committee of U.S.A.): ed. Shervin B. Hawley
World Order (National Spiritual Assembly of the Bahá'ís of the United States): poetry ed. Robert Hayden

ISBN 0–85398–108–6 (cased)
ISBN 0–85398–109–4 (paper)

I beseech Thee . . . not to withhold from us the things Thou hast irrevocably ordained in this Revelation . . . that hath enabled every least pebble to resound again with Thy praise, as the stones glorified Thee in the days of Muḥammad, Thy Friend

Bahá'u'lláh

In loving tribute to all who
witness
in life or in death

CONTENTS

INTRODUCTION

All things fall and are built again,
And those that build them again are gay.

W. B. Yeats

The success of Roger White's first volume of poems, *Another Song, Another Season,* has prepared the way for this present offering. The new volume is amply provided with panegyrics of known and unidentified Bahá'ís and is full of the spirit of tolerance and aspiration that animates the Bahá'í revelation. For truly, if poetry, in a short line, can give more life to history than grand tomes crammed with commentary and research, we see it here.

But it would be a pity if the distinctive poetic voice of our 'Bahá'í Laureate' were lost sight of in initial enthusiasm at finding Bahá'í saints, heroes and episodes portrayed in verse. As fine and sensitive a poet as Roger White does not write poetry to project his own personality, it is true. But the mind of a poet is to be found at its most diffuse within the poetic creation, and the mind of Roger White is a deft, deceptively insinuating quotient.

First, it is evident that he is a religious poet. Possibly no one since Herbert has written with the same lyricism about the love of God:

Love offers first the suppliant at its gate
faith's bricks and planks and rusted nails that wound.
To fragile shelter built to love's spare plan,
gold-laden, comes royal lover's caravan.

Yet the quality of religious feeling we find in Roger White's poems is not over-ethereal or etherized. It is good to find a Bahá'í poet giving the cypress trees and rivers a rest, and including the raw material of life, as well as its up-surging, within the compass of a religious vision. We might say he has admitted all the random sordidness, vulgarity, loneliness and despair, but seen it transfused with a golden seam of intense joy. The modernist takes the same raw data but yearns for disengagement; Roger White's unsettling commitment is not to fierce ideals and the worst form of passionate intensity. The story of every poem is almost too simple, too naïve, to be of this century. Yet with what a bitter-joyfulness is it expressed: the cesspool of the world has not marred a still child-like consciousness of the kingdom of heaven:

Excess of joy, he gave as explanation.

This simplicity is not, however, bereft of a wry, disarming radicalism, that looks askance at shibboleths new and old, and subtly reminds us that such things arise within our very own selves. Thus the story of Zalina, where the nickel does not change its mint at the wish of the self-appointed cambio man:

My own sense of theatre would prefer the glib ending. I would have chosen to have had Zalina, with Hollywood presto-chango flair, embrace the Bahá'í Cause with fervour, give up her worldly ways and go pioneering to some remote outpost where she would have lived in a maximum of physical discomfort—malaria, of course, a pestilential climate, and man-eating crocodiles . . .

The deep insight into the virtues of the human heart which we find in Roger White's poetry uncovers a brighter world than that of Ibsen or Dostoyevsky, a world so rarely explored in literature, where the potential for good within the human soul is realized. Time and again we find the poet loving human beings, though their sins be scarlet. There is indignation in this volume, but not hatred; awareness of falsity, but not dualism. In the stiff-upper-lip English lady, the egregious American tart, the unlettered Arab workman, and 'languageless' Israeli—in all it is the good which is discovered. We can imagine a little how 'Abdu'l-Bahá read the heart of every individual, every face.

Surely it is a very great achievement to look at life, to see it whole, and ultimately to face, not despair but joy? The modern age desperately needs to learn this secret, to rediscover, as our poet has done, that the essence of life is not complexity, not tragedy, but simple truth. Yet all is turned inside out, and we writhe to wear our hair shirt not believing it possible to change it for one that does not gall and lacerate.

Roger White has shown that the many-coloured coat of the brotherhood of man, made of the love of God and the sacrifice of heroic souls in the name of hope and peace, is the only one fit for our brothers and sisters to wear:

I saw gardens bloom in desert sand,
A singing man who had been dumb,
A bell that pealed without a tongue,
A witless scholar once well versed
Whose Order yields a world reversed?

Geoffrey Nash

PART ONE:

THE WITNESS OF PEBBLES:
POEMS AND PORTRAYALS

The contemptuous and self-regarding mountains
haughty in glacial ermine
shrugged Dawn from their sleek height
from which it sank to play upon
the dull and earnest pebbles. These
drank in clumsy wonder the rising light
marvelling that they—
so slight a thing, unfaceted
and dun and porous—
should grow luminous and warm with day.

Were they to speak
what might they chorus
but The Sun! The Sun!

Roger White

THE TRUE BROTHER

You . . .
across the Twin resplendent seas
which cast this pearl
we ask what praise
is adequate to you?

You . . .
who knew far more than we
how little was the little
that we knew.

You . . .
rescued from despondency
by the audacious exploits
of so few.

You . . .
how belatedly we see
that you were more than brother,
more than true.

You . . .
through a mercy
we've not earned O! comfort us
who did not comfort
you . . .

THE HELPMATE

We affirm the symbol,
would not wish removal of the
protective, important and necessary lace
which unsuited by fragility and function
so little veiled her
from fate's iron lacerations;
but, unstraining, see
beyond the radiant power
the educable woman,
maker of bread,
the sonsy, glad and practical girl
who came obediently,
pearl of the pearl,
to her various cogent sorrows.

. . . my helpmate, my shield,
my tireless collaborator . . .

Do not think, Montreal,
the joy, the honour, the anguish
less real
for awareness of history's hunkered spectre
brooding watchfully in the shadows.

Let us imagine
the accolades of angels
in her ultimate and unique desolation
who knew
much, much more than we
our loss.
Someone had to bear the unbearable
for an unknowing world.
Not every heart supports a golden eagle.

Through a white and private mist,
smiling for our consolation,
she moves as queens are trained
and peasants immemorially have known to do
tutored by pain
but oh, the veil,
the veil and train are heavy;
we cannot know their weight!

Although the vital, slender hands
command audaciously,
call us acutely to untried heights,
we see the lorn, vulnerable fingers,
restive and unreconciled and unredressed,
beating like torn wings
among the roses
which drown in scarlet helplessness
at the marble column's foot.

(*Sonsy:* Scot., luck-bringing, comely, comfortable-looking good-natured;
from Gaelic *sonas*, good luck. See note, p. 201.)

A WHISPERED EPITAPH

John E. Esslemont
(1874–1925)

. . . the Scottish disciple of 'Abdu'l-Bahá . . .

Much may be made of a Scotchman if he be caught young.
Samuel Johnson 1709–1784

Here at the foot of Carmel
where the simple stones are arrayed
to publish heaven's humble handful
it is as though a hovering presence
in this cradling shade
were whispering . . . *of this one much was made.*
Caught young enough to prosper
he became the stuff
which furnishes hero, servant, gentleman.
   Carved by an unknown hand the words:
     By all who knew him he was loved.

Or if supine slabbed witness were not trusted
turn to the canny neutral trees,
the cypress, eucalyptus, palm and pine.
Mark how, serene and mute and grizzled,
they lean in slender ease
and drop across his chiselled name
their suspiring silver-dusted leaves
like young girls strewing floral tribute.
Were they to speak might not they tell . . .
    This bonny lad did well . . .

GEORGE TOWNSHEND
1876–1957

Leave the bells, and come forth, then, from your churches . . . The divine who hath seized and quaffed the most holy Wine, in the name of the sovereign Ordainer, is an eye unto the world. Well is it with them who . . . call him to remembrance.

Bahá'u'lláh

> *God passes by.* And you,
> having dreamed an Ireland
> greener than she knew,
> marked His footprint
> in the sleeping vineyard,
> saw the grapes renew.
> Not law nor literature
> nor steepled creed
> could stay you from becoming
> bell of the Most Great Bell
> to plead *Awake! Awake!*
> The injured island
> kept its silent wake.
>
> Observe us now,
> intemperate with recognition,
> seize the raddling cup of gladdening brew,
> cross the bridge
> your exquisite anguish drew
> to the Jerusalem your hopes had peopled.
>
> Hear us, pausing at the wide-flung gate,
> exclaim in awe—
>   *This* the heaven,
>   *this* the earth he saw.
>
> A quick light silvery laugh rings out;
> the voice is gay.
> *And would that be yerselves?* we hear you say.

OLYMPIC CHAMPION
Agnes Baldwin Alexander
1875–1971

It was a little disconcerting trying to round up Agnes Alexander to discuss a fixed agenda. 'You run along and consult, dearie.' she'd say, sweetly, 'I've had my guidance for today from 'Abdu'l-Bahá—and she'd skip off.

(remark by a contemporary)

This is an unlikely Olympian—
one might have thought
she had taken a correspondence course
in how to be a sweet little old lady.
Or Helen Hokinson might have created her—
a few deft lines would have fixed
the twinkling eyes,
the springing sausage curls.

Everything she wears speaks
of respectability,
would give access to Schrafft's,
the opera, the civic meeting,
the literary tea,
the ocean cruise:
the clubwoman's flowered hat,
the well-cut anonymous print,
a smug servant of mobility—
one sees it drip-drying in
crushproof decorum,
tediously serviceable,
ready to invade the lobby
of the imposing hotel.
Her face would pose no problem
for the artist,
a face where winsome tutored submission
and girlish rebellion
find reconciliation.

What will the artist make of this?
Stepping from the motor car
with an energy that overleaps
the frail and wasting frame
the woman pauses.
On boyscout impulse
you extend your sturdy arm
and win affectionate admonishment:
    Dearie! Do you think my Lord does not guide my step?

She skitters into sunlight,
your useless strength outwitted.
You know yourself delightfully outdistanced,
compellingly instructed,
grateful,
as you stumble after her
adoringly.

Unquestionably, some old ladies
know a trick or two
about where to plant the feet.

CONSOLATION PIECE

for Enoch Olinga
1927–1979

The commodious mind again assaulted
reluctantly accommodates yet another violent image,
the family gunned down in flight,
the shattered forms sprawled gauchely,
as forbiddingly withdrawn from life as children
who in their mysterious, earnest sleep
are locked from us in an exclusive privacy
that arrests our tiptoe visit to the darkened room
flooding us with reverence
and sudden distaste for our heart's own beat.

And oh, the aimless blood
gathering in silent pools of accusation!
We would retreat reeling from this havoc
as from a hundred other impinged atrocities
to posture philosophically from an impersonal distance
before faith's flattering mirror
where we preen our self-esteem in congratulatory composure;
but having known them, sharing their vision,
we are left with rising gorge in a stone calm
in which indignation and acquiescence battle.

Does this blood accuse the world
which does not know, or we who do
and yet have done so little? Tomorrow
we shall weep for the death of innocents,
speak haltingly of sacrifice,
ask ourselves what time is left
and what is ransomed here.

But now, against the madness,
before the habile hagiographers unleash their spate,
let the mind cast up consoling recollection:
a Kampalan traditional welcome,
the compelling music of cowhide drums,
five hundred figures responding in agitative abandon
and in their midst a magnificent black and glistening male
surrendered from his station
to move in the imperative language of dance,
not as tranced martyrs move,
but in a purely human ecstasy.
And laughing, brothers, laughing.

DANCING-MASTER

In Memoriam: Raḥmatu'lláh Muhájir

Today, to this melody of the Company on high, the world will leap and dance . . . But know ye this: Save for this song of God, no song will stir the world.

'Abdu'l-Bahá

Posterity will record his devoted services . . . unique exploits . . . ceaseless efforts . . . his exemplary unflagging zeal . . .

The Universal House of Justice
30 December 1979

Remark the many dancers, how they sweep and swing
Who had no cause to dance, were mute and still
But, lissome in light-limbed freedom, now wing,
Whirl and dart in unrandom ecstasy. Will
We recognize no pattern in their tread
And think them witless puppets unfit to weave
Heaven's measured gleeful figure? Woodenly dead,
The stringed doll would not smile so, nor its bosom heave.
These come gladly to the gala and gladder grow
Till gaining in abandonment one lithe leaper blur,
Masterfully incandescent, in a blink's span go,
Called into the darling refrain, our foot's gay spur.
One leaves, just so. Fairer for this, and sweeter,
The globe-stirring grace-note— the dancers fleeter.

HISTORY LESSON

In Memoriam: H. M. Balyuzí
1908–1980

If thou art a man of learning, thy knowledge becometh an honour, and if thou art a follower, thine adherence unto leadership becometh an honour, only when these conform to the good-pleasure of God.

The Báb

Summoned to tea in Hampstead
I found the setting for a savant,
the room monochromatic,
the books many and in meticulous disarray,
your kindly urbane face
the brightest object in that study.

Pain had softened the aristocratic outline
permitting your presence to loom
gently overshadowing the flesh
which seemed supported by an inflexible integrity,
your will pinned furiously to one awesome purpose,
the writing of that Life.

In the stage invalid's articulate costume
of surrender to infirmity,
a robe anonymously plaid
and worn with an accustomed resignation,
yours was a fragrance not of medicines.
You wore achievement lightly as a lap-robe
with an inborn graciousness, a princely ease.

Your quiet voice described the outline of your book
in a scholar's subdued excitement
but the hand in subtle motion was an artist's.
Many the mantles you might have worn,
I thought, but saw the pawn exacted by good-pleasure.

The panorama of the mountain
must not blind one to the pebble.
A private path had brought you
to this truth.

Later, when you had spoken with radiant intensity
of minutiae of the life of some obscure believer
we sat smiling at each other in silence
neglectful of the coursing tears
cooling with our tea.

London: October 1978

POSY

In Memoriam: Adelbert Mühlschlegel

His great humility almost blinded one to his many accomplishments, not the least of these being his poems which he referred to, with charming diffidence, as his 'little posies.'

(tribute by a contemporary)

True modesty admits of no disguise;
Like an unalterable mountain it will rise
Commanding our eye with supreme surprise.
All that the crags give life we but surmise.

Let us conjecture the summit from the flowers,
The shyest tokens, sprung from casual hours
Almost unnoticed on the slope where the pine towers.
Their fragrance hints the peak may yet be ours.

We seize them up to read the humble brief,
Find spelled in hardy petal, root and leaf
The alphabets that bloom into belief
Doubt's frost can't blight nor winter wrap in grief.

All this the posies speak; what more tip's snows
Mirroring light to Light as daybreak grows?

IN MEMORIAM: A. Q. Faizi
1906–1980

A special sweetness has gone out of the world . . .
William Sears

The children by the upturned sod
strew flowers, weeping. Only God
Who holds the slightest winged thing dear
knows all the sweetness folded here.
Were such love possible? ask we
who dole it with economy,
squander doubt and hoard affection
in private vaults beyond detection.

On Carmel trails the sun's gilt sleeve
as we chilled mourners slowly leave
and to a lessened warmth then turn
who tutored by our loss might learn
to seize the thought this death installs:
who'd serve the King must love His thralls.

LINES FOR A WOMAN OF YAZD

*What we have sacrificed in the path of God
no man has the right to return to us.*
(Words addressed by the mother of the young martyr, 'Alí-Aṣghar
Shahíd of Yazd, to his executioners to whom she returned the
severed head of her son which they had cast before her and his bride.)

Intent upon his devotions
or his bride's deft grace
as she bent swiftly to the samovar
he could not have imagined Carmel
half a century hence
or our complacent town, a church on every corner,

Shakespeare an academic rumour irrelevant
to our fathers who ran the trains,
and Islám disposed of in the locker room
by smirking seniors avid for pinups
but not yet for compassion or forgiveness.

We did not conceive of being lovable
as we applied our power to modest uses
and formulaic pieties,
drifting through conventional peurilities
into jobs, marriages and well-meant assignations,
improvising our lives from movies and pulp fiction,
tamping down our hunger with furtive
readings of Gibran whose diluted distillations
did not satiate the self ravenous for reality
or rid our populous dreams
of extreme and unnamed heroes.
We who reserved roses for funerals
and the graduation prom corsage
had never seen a nightingale.

How, even now, to make his swift trajection real
or voice our opsimathic wonder that one so young
could be so careless of corporeality?
Yet he is given us forever in his mother's words.

Sorrowing opaquely for his cruel curtailment
could she have known that
down the long dark decades
he should be needed calamitously dead
that we, adroitly trifling with illusions,
might grasp the vivid reason why we live?

What might you have chosen, mother, for your boy—
an obscure and virtuous longevity or
this rare and self-renewing veneration?

Take comfort, woman of Yazd.
Even in our town, now, they speak his name in awe.

HEAVEN'S FOOL

Ḥájí 'Abdu'l-Majíd (Abá Badí')

We marvel at the spirit of renunciation that prompted those sore pressed sufferers . . . that induced the father of Badí', one of that gallant company, to fling unhesitatingly by the roadside the satchel, full of turquoises which he had brought from his father's mine in Níshápúr . . .

Shogi Effendi
God Passes By

See it for what it was, the smallest part,
The least response to what was asked that day.
It was my reason that I cast away.
Has he need of turquoise who has lost his heart?
If the act informs of virtue, understand
It was the glad taking on of madness— this
Speaks. As from love-besotted lips speeds kiss
So did the gem bag lightly leave my hand.
See it as it was, then, a trifling thing:
As breath released, so was the satchel hurled
And with it— here the better truth!— the world.
Laud lover's zeal, not short-lived rose he flings.
They name me well who count me heaven's fool,
Know recompense for stone was rarer jewel.

THE UNCHAINED TONGUE

—the song of <u>Sh</u>ay<u>kh</u> 'Alí-Akbar-i-Mázgání—

*By disposition and because of the intense love in his heart [for Bahá'u'lláh],
he yearned to write poetry, to fashion odes and __ghazals__, but he lacked both
metre and rhyme.*

'Abdu'l-Bahá

Was all said by the ancients, those whose praise
Of vanished beauty looms as yet to cower
The honour we would heap upon the hour
Leased us? The crippled verse, the floundering phrase
Dash on stone lips at thought of their great odes
Of heroes, love requited, faith reprieved,
Repair of hope, the heart exulting unaggrieved,
The soul's quest for Desired One's abode.
The tongue is chained at memory of each word
Wrested from agile joy or bruising pain,
Sprung from spirit's vast spectrum, song-thronged brain.
The golden-voiced spoke; it is absurd
I not be mute who know no song be new
Or unsurpassed. Yet must I tell of You.

THE COMFORTER

Myrta (Perkins) Swingle, 1876–1962, accepted the Bahá'í Faith in Cleveland, Ohio circa 1905, as a result of hearing Percy Woodcock, an early Canadian believer, describe his recent pilgrimage to 'Akká where he met 'Abdu'l-Bahá. When the Master visited Chicago in 1912, Myrta attained His presence on several occasions; later He spoke at her home in Cleveland. Once in Chicago, she went to His room in the Plaza Hotel and learning that the Master was visiting the friends elsewhere she was overcome with an impulse to enter the room, climb upon the bed and cradle 'Abdu'l-Bahá's blanket about her. Later she said of this: 'I did not know then the spiritual significance of that gesture!'

The girl grew wiser, of course,
and with the deep wisdom, older;
then would not creep into the room colder
for absence of the warmth
she'd felt enfold her—
reunion's glowing coals—
and growing bolder,
childishly curl, undetected,
draw across her trembling shoulder
the blanket He had touched
(for her perfected).

Had her discovery been effected
(the entourage outraged
at the uncalculating tableau
love had wildly staged?)
would He scold her mildly,
perhaps have told her
that cloaked and protected
by His titles, above all comforters
the Covenant would hold her?

Or might we think that He
Who beyond our guessing
knew symbol as the soul's mute tongue
would have smiled
above her dreaming form,
her hand guilelessly outflung,
and breathed in blessing:
Rest here, my child.
(Was ever one so warm?)

IN MEMORIAM: Margery McCormick

1889–1964

*Love only what you do,
and not what you have done.*

Adrienne Rich
The Diamond Cutter

You preferred to wear out than rust out
and were in constant motion,
your faith homely as a brown-bag lunch,
a selected goodness.
Your loaves-and-fishes wonder
familiarized the miracle,
piqued even jaded palates.

And if the rented halls were empty
still you spoke, released into the ether
the Most Great Name, your own heart kindling.
We who heard you were returned
to a vision of our own perfectibility
relinquished when we gratefully resigned to limitation.
The good broth of your speech nourished many.

And drew blame as well as praise,
greater in measure for your lack of interest,
indifferent as a magnet
to the filings it compels.

But knew them dangerous.
Brushed them from your shoulder like snow,
scooped and balled them playfully
to cast behind you into the Ocean
where they melted harmlessly.

You wound down at last
with the simplicity of a child's model plane
but were in motion till the end, unrusted,
loving the flight,
no ice on your wings.

REGINALD TURVEY: 1882–1968

Spiritual Father of South Africa

Our greed did not dismay him
nor all the monuments we raised to gold
nor the confused virtue we enforced
with our bibles and our whips.
His ferny dreams did not spawn diamonds;
they were not drenched with blood
or spangled with the blackman's sweat.

He spoke with paint
in tones as quiet as his hope,
wry as his smile,
his life, his work unattended
by our notice or acclaim.
But all shall know this man in time,
in a distant hour
when our cities have grown silent,
when our scorched eyes
have lifted in terror
and our power has seeped away
as from an open vein.

The complacent sons of sundowners
will blink in amazed recognition
crying 'You!'
and the tunnelling millions
who bear on their backs
the weight of our towers and tyranny
will step proudly into light
exclaiming 'Father! Our little Father!'
Good, they will call him, good,
the white and the black
and all the other brothers, every one.

Time will reveal him
and songs will sound to celebrate his name
in a future hour
in a time which heaven hastens.

We shall gaze in wonder
at the love
thick on his dried brushes.

'Might this have saved us?' we shall ask,
needing no answer.

THE GIFT

Curtis DeMude Kelsey
1894–1970

In 1921 Curtis Kelsey was summoned to the Holy Land to illuminate the Holy Shrines at the request of 'Abdu'l-Bahá. On one occasion the Master summoned Curtis into His room, had him sit opposite Him, and just looked into his eyes for several minutes, not saying anything. Curtis could not stop returning the Master's gaze. Then the Master smiled His wonderful smile and dismissed him. It was some time before Curtis realized the meaning of that incident, but as the years passed the face of 'Abdu'l-Bahá would always appear to him in moments of difficulty and his problems would seem smaller.

'In Memoriam'
The Bahá'í World
vol. XV

With that face given to me had I need
Of other gift? With those eyes holding mine
The shrivelled earth lost power to incline
Me to its shimmering mirage, to heed
Its ashy course, its dimming stars' design—
In one long glance the light of sun was mine!
Embossed on all my days this best of gifts,
A compelling image rising in my brain
To challenge me to virtue past my reach.
Thus comforted, upheld, the frail heart lifts
To meet the imprinted living goad again
And pluck sweet victory like the low-hung peach.
His countenance held heaven's very plan.
That message read, what other need I scan?

DISTINCTION

'Abdu'l-Bahá said the only difference between Him and us was that He was dependent on Bahá'u'lláh every instant, and we sometimes forget.

Curtis DeMude Kelsey

Behold a candle how it gives its light. It weeps its life away drop by drop in order to give forth its flame of light.

'Abdu'l-Bahá

With every breath to celebrate breath's source:
Was merely this the perspicuous distinction,
To be as choiceless candle hastening extinction,
Burning with single purpose its brief course
Mindful of the wick, the hand that set the flame,
The oxygen it drinks to speed its end,
Casting its light for stranger and for friend
Nor caring were one beautiful, another plain?
Is this the model consciously we'd choose?
The faithless mind contrives a thousand ways
To fit distraction to our fleeting days
Yet sorrows for the unnamed thing we lose.
What use were lungs unless in every breath
Life's source be remembered? Were all else death?

INDIAN SUMMER

Alfred James Loft (1908–1973) was the first Canadian Bahá'í of the Mohawk tribe. His earliest childhood recollection was of sitting on a fence near his home in Tyendinaga, Ontario watching a train crossing the landscape. A figure clothed in flowing white robes was on the train, smiling and waving at him. In confusion and delight Jim toppled backwards. When he found the Bahá'í Faith in 1948 he recognized the figure on the train as 'Abdu'l-Bahá Who had left Montreal on 9 September 1912 on a train bound for Toronto where He changed trains for Buffalo, New York. In 1949, in obedience to Shoghi Effendi's wishes, Jim returned with his family to Tyendinaga to establish the Faith among his people, remaining there until his death.

The crickets drenched the field with sound
Each tree branch wore a crow
While soft September sunlight wound
The whole in lazy bow

And noosed in it the Mohawk's dream
Where he, astride the fence,
Surveyed the hazy autumn scene
In moccasined suspense

Till toppled from his perch by what
Then overtook his brain:
Perfection seen tied in that knot
And waving from a train.

The heart ensnared thus none can free
For only One unravels
Grosgrain spun of eternity
By Love in its swift travels.

RECOGNITION
For Allan Raynor

Death was that exotic thing
that glamorized the idols of your adolesence
who met it young, as an ideal favour,
as though in fulfilment of your romantic need,
a refined and lace-edged matter,
Keatsian or Chopinesque;
or heroic— an unmarked grave on foreign soil,
achieved in some unnamed doomed crusade.

Sometimes it was a neighbourhood affair,
unmemorable as a family meal,
someone's chimney-corner grandparent or relation
slipping soundlessly away,
the parts worn out or ambushed by disuse,
poignancy blunted by nonimmortal domesticity.

Usually it was irrelevant
like the earthquakes and civil disasters
visited upon the remote anonymous
Chinese or Guatemalans you saw in newsreels,
their pale flickering anguish less real
than the smell of dust and plush,
the taste of buttered popcorn.

Later, with the passing of companions
succumbing undramatically in quiet valour
under antiseptic surveillance
in their suburban beds,
you see it as it must always have been,
genial and undemanding
like the grocer's silent, serviceable wife
propped patiently and unnoticed behind the till
whose familiar presence startles you
into belated recognition.

Do come again, dear, she says
with a pleasant, knowing smile,
looking up from her unerring tally.

I will, I will! you say
as to a valued friend
to whom you owe a duty,
gratefully pledging your custom
to her immaculate and undiscriminating constancy.

PAUSING

In Memoriam: Robert Hayden
1913–1980

Above all other black poets in the United States he has managed to create out of the painful reality of blackness . . . sophisticated word-structures which are both intensely personal and completely universal . . .

Paul Breman
You Better Believe It
(Penguin anthology of verse in English by black poets, 1973)

Pause, now, to salute this man
Who tamed his pain and made it scan;

Who knew entitlement of rage
But sweetened it upon the page,

Spelled our forgiveness for his race
Whose tortures had that gift erased.

Above a dying epoch's shriek
He took the human risk to speak

As though we had not murdered trust
And left love bleeding in the dust.

We praise black courage as we tread
White with awe by his green bed.

Too soon compassion for man's guilt
Lies stilled beneath our common quilt.

A PLACE BEYOND

In some countries of the world where, even today, Bahá'ís are imprisoned for their faith, various efforts are employed to induce them to recant including, in the case of women, sanctioned and repeated rape.

My sour-breathed defiler
brings to his sweating, earnest task
an almost holy anger.
Remote in his rage, unsmiling,
he joylessly enacts upon my dumb and vulnerable body
the traditional violation
he cannot perpetrate against my chaste steel mind.

I am placed beyond this vileness.
Hot and flushed,
made mythical by intensity,
he labours over me,
abstract as an animal.
His coarsest invectives,
harmless as petals,
brush against my balking, distant soul.
Hollowly, a world apart from my immaculate privacy,
his spasmed groan announces
the profundity of his defeat.
How pitiful, after all,
as means of profanation,
the perverse ritual,
the vaunted, swift-shrunk telescope of lust.

He wrenches away
rancidly liquid,
clumsily fumbling,
administers a parting kick.
My cheek scraped raw by his abradant beard
receives his spittle,
the pathetic final coin of his contempt
that does not buy his lost dignity.

The cell door rasps in metallic obeisance
before the ox-like form;
I hear his arrogant ribald boast
to the indifferent, disbelieving guards.

Soon I shall reclaim my stunned and stubborn flesh,
rise from this obfuscation dry-eyed
to attend my pain and bruises.
No stoic, I. But given this
I shall accept it as a benediction;
unabashed, I offer this as yet another prayer.

Dry-eyed, I say. No longer do I weep
and cringe and scream aloud; mutely
withhold such sought-for titillation.
I grow familiar with humiliation,
ask to endure with honour
as might the dust the tyrant's heel
or holy book the torch set by fanatic.
I shall not buy release with recantation.

I know your torment, tormentor. Your
humid eyes invade obscenely my dark dreams
where hate festers, but you are not my victor
nor I despoiled
while I forgive— yes, even this.

My poor, my sad, my lonely brother!
I yet shall see you break against
the wall of my endurance,
drown in self-disgust
before my inviolate, annulling gaze.

O Thou my Shield and Shelter,
in Whose Name all suffering is borne,
comfort me,
conceal my shame with the cloak of Thy compassion
and grant that in Thy realm
this sorrow be my robe of immortality . . .

NO

The incident described occurred in 1979 when a hostile mob entered the home of an old shepherd and his wife, Bahá'ís of a small village in Írán, demanding under threat of death by fire that they recant their faith. The poem is based on the husband's reply which turned the mob away. On 19 May 1980 the old shepherd was found dead, having been stoned to death while tending his flock. To reveal the names at this time might further endanger lives.

I

You may have our lives. It is no great feat
To slay us, we are simply flesh and bone.
Here is my wife, my children, our home;
Here too the kindling, there the ready flame.
With your contempt to feed and fan the heat
We will quickly fall to ash and our name
Soon vanish from the village. But to buy breath
With denial would be shabbier death.
Strike the match, then, if that is your desire.
What shall we fear who know Undying Fire?

II

Make room in some slim volume
for his rustic words which
unlike the politicians' pious exhortations
did not grace
the headlines of our tabloid day.
No: it is little enough to say
but literature and legends will grow
from this and our true, our other history
give it place.
Salute the mystery:
his *No*—empowered to dismay—
dissolves our reservations
to reserve us heaven,
survives to erase
the impudent smirk from Death's
irrelevant face.

BROKEN SILENCE

. . . a score of Bahá'í Holy Places [in Írán] have been destroyed or confiscated by the local authorities, centres of worship in eighty towns and villages have been destroyed or burned down, some forty cemeteries have been profaned, and in most cases confiscated . . .

Eric Rouleau
Le Monde: 29 August 1980

Blameless and derelict the outworn bones lie uselessly
where the vanished flesh forsook them,
the habitants urged past our mourning and memory
toward an unimaginable destination.
Soon none might remember their uneventful decency,
none regret the servitors' docile passage
to anonymity, who had done with us and
asked no larger kindness, yet will serve us once again.

We see you strain in furious ambition
to erase the homely graves which were content
to hold their silence,
find voice to ask what was the potent preference
of these untenanted relics
that your fear should war upon it
even in the tolerant annulling dust
which patiently abides to cover you?

ARNOS GROVE

Arnos Grove is the station on the London subway from which access is gained to the resting place of Shoghi Effendi in the Great Northern London Cemetery at New Southgate.

She is old and unabashedly English
and undeceived by the thin spring sunlight
uncompromisingly wears worn self-caricaturizing tweed.
Her brisk stride brooks no nonsense
stakes ownership
seems to hold the very street in place.

Sparrow-bright her head tilts to my question
betrays an interest belied by the reply
clipped neatly as a privet hedge.

>   *Straight on to the circle then*
>   *bear right through Brunswick Mews to the gate.*

She hovers, cocked to my foreignness.
and risks the impropriety

>   *You're young to be visiting a cemetery.*
>   *Someone you love?*

Love and honour, I aver, marvelling
that reverence be so domestically compressed.
Her eyes peck briefly at the unexpressed
and misting swivel toward the solid slab of road
sweep the resolutely decorous shopfronts.

> *They're lovely to visit, the dead.*
> *So still, and yet not lonely.*
> *Each year I feel a little closer . . .*

A trained restraint chokes off the rush of words.
She bustles away, unthanked,
skimming raggedly as on a vagrant wind
past a dense cluster of sluggish shoppers
intent on meagre errands.

Now, diminishing, only her purposeful shopping bag
bulging with pedestrian purchases
seems to secure her to earth.

THE INDISCRETION OF
MARIE-THÉRÈSE BEAUCHAMPS

The time of the sojourn was limited to a number of days, but the results in the future are inexhaustible.

'Abdu'l-Bahá

Loretteville, Québec
1 September 1962

Ah Beauchamps, you were married to a fool, and if you ever doubted it you know it now; at my age to be making this long journey to Montreal, just to see the place again. But I do this, Jean Paul, for both of us for I derive more comfort there than from the

Masses I have said for you. It brings you close; it helps me remember how it was between us when we were just beginning our life together, before the children came. There I do not feel the sadness I experience when I tend your grave. Sometimes I cry a little, but for a different cause. Grant me my little solace, Beauchamps, and be patient with an old fool. Forgive me, too, for having kept this from you all these years— the only secret I ever withheld from you who knew me like your own hand. It was not a matter for the confessional but I would defend it before the Mother of God who surely knows my heart. It is a bitter thing to outlive so many of those you have loved.

It is different now, I must remember, with half the building torn down. I must prepare myself for that. I always expect it will look the same as when I first saw it so many years ago. I was a shy and awkward girl and would not have dared approach so grand a place, but it drew me like a magnet for I had seen a picture of that face. I have often wondered whether it was by accident that I glimpsed the newspaper. The photograph leapt out at me, the face as familiar as the face of my father. My heart was pierced by those eyes. I could not struggle with the print but asked my friend who reads English to explain. Such stories she told! The papers had been full of the news of his arrival, his sermons. He was called the Apostle of Peace. 'He is an Eastern Sage,' my friend said, but my heart told me that he was much more than that, though who or what he might be, I could not tell. The Aunt of my friend knew someone whose child had been healed by his touch. He was a worker of miracles. Oh Beauchamps, I needed a miracle. Three years married and my womb still barren. My tears, my novenas, the votive lamps— nothing availed. Mother of Heaven let me see him! I prayed.

It was easy to find the Windsor Hotel. A crowd had gathered and I stood unnoticed at the edge, not nervous but shaking with excitement, and feeling shabby and out of place among those elegant people, among *les anglais*. But when he arrived I felt no strangeness, just great awe and a tender love, for he shone, Beauchamps, with a beautiful light. He had the face of a saint which held all the happiness of heaven and all the sorrowful burdens of earth. No one saw me as I quickly crossed myself in his holy presence.

But then a deep shame swept over me as I watched him move among the people, smiling and greeting them, for they were like children, each wanting the attention of their tired and patient father, each wanting a solution to their problems, an answer to their questions and their needs, just as I did. I wanted to leave but I could not turn away from his gleaming figure. He will know no rest, I thought. We will crucify him with our questions. We all want to take from him but who will help him in his great work? God strengthen him for this, I prayed silently.

At that moment, almost as though I had called his name, he turned his glance in my direction and for the first time I felt the full force of his gaze. There are no words to describe it, my Jean Paul, but it was as though he read the pages of my soul. My heart which had been pounding wildly was overcome with a greater peace than I have ever known. There was in his glance all the sad wisdom and tenderness that must have been seen in the face of Our Lord, and a question, too, but I could not read it. The moment seemed like eternity.

Then he smiled and turned to reply to someone who spoke to him and I knew what I would do. I had to touch him, just lightly touch his robe. I still do not know whether it was courage or madness that prompted me, but I had no willpower to resist that impulse.

I made my way through the crowd quietly and unobserved. Who would notice anyone while that holy man was in their midst! Closer I came until I could almost reach out and touch him. And then the woman in front of me who had been speaking to him began to weep softly and in turning away she stepped aside and I was face to face with him. Without thinking of what I was doing I began to genuflect in order to touch the hem of his robe to my lips but he caught my arm and raised me to my feet and held my gaze searchingly. My both hands were in his. I do not know what language he spoke but I understood his gentle words: No, my daughter. He reached into his pocket with a swift grace and pressed something into my palm with a playful smile and released me without a word, easing himself away so smoothly that my little indiscretion had scarcely been noticed and caused no embarrassment.

I slipped away then, stepping backward slowly through the people who were glad enough to come forward to replace me, and then I began to run across the square, stopping for breath under the trees where I continued to watch for a little while until he entered the building and the crowd drifted away. Only then did I remember that he had placed in my hand the gift which I still held in my clenched fingers. Two little sweets wrapped in paper. I did not doubt what they were for. They were our banquet that night, Jean Paul.

When I conceived Pierre I was tempted to tell you, but how could I have found the words? And then the other children came and there was no need to speak of it for life moved on in the normal way. How gladly I gave Pierre and Martine to the church, and would have willingly seen the others take Holy Orders, too, if they had had the call. And so I never spoke to you of this, my Beauchamps. Do you smile from heaven as you watch me come here each year on this day to offer gratitude?

Sometimes I think the grandchildren might understand if I were to speak of it, especially Céleste, who is like one of God's angels. Perhaps I will speak of it to her one day and bring her along; I would be glad of her company on the bus. We could sit under the trees in the square and I could try to describe him to her. But what shall I say if she asks what became of the Apostle of Peace for I never saw him again or heard what became of his work. But I know it was the work of God and God's work is not lost even after half a century.

Will Céleste laugh at the pilgrimage of a stupid old woman? No, she will try to understand. She has my ways, but is more restless, more questing, and finds no answers in the church. She reads about the Buddha and Muhammad— matters we did not speak of in my day. No, Céleste will not mock the stranger work of heaven.

L'INDISCRETION DE
MARIE-THÉRÈSE BEAUCHAMPS

La durée du séjour était limitée à quelques heures, mais les résultats dans le futur seront inépuisables.

'Abdu'l-Bahá

Loretteville, Québec
1er *Septembre 1962*

Ben oui, Beauchamps, tu étais marié à une folle et si tu en as jamais douté, tu le sais maintenant: à mon âge, faire ce long voyage à Montréal juste pour revoir l'endroit. Mais ceci, Jean-Paul, je le fais pour nous deux car je ressens plus de réconfort là-bas qu'aux messes que j'ai fait dire pour toi. Ça te ramène près de moi. Ça m'aide à me rappeler comment c'était entre nous tout au début de notre vie à deux, avant l'arrivée des enfants. Là-bas, je ne ressens pas de tristesse comme quand j'entretiens ta tombe. Des fois, je pleure un peu, mais pour une toute autre raison. Donne-moi un peu de réconfort, Beauchamps, et sois patient avec une vieille folle. Pardonne-moi aussi de t'avoir caché ce secret pendant toutes ces années. C'était le seul que je ne t'avais pas dit, à toi qui me connaissais si bien. Ce secret n'est pas quelque chose à dire au confessionnal mais je le défendrais devant la Mère de Dieu qui connaît sûrement mon coeur.

C'est une chose amère que de survivre à tant de gens que l'on a aimés . . . Il faut dire que c'est différent maintenant que la moitié de l'hôtel a été démolie. Je dois m'y préparer. Je m'attends toujours à ce qu'il ait la même apparence que la première fois que je l'ai vu, il y a tant d'années. J'étais alors une fille timide et gauche et je n'aurais jamais osé m'approcher d'un endroit si magnifique, mais j'étais comme attirée par un aimant après avoir vu une photographie de ce visage. Je me suis souvent demandé si c'était par hasard que j'avais jeté un coup d'oeil au journal. L'image m'avait sauté aux yeux: le visage m'était aussi familier que celui de mon père, mon coeur avait été transpercé par ces yeux. Je n'arrivais pas à comprendre le texte alors j'ai demandé à mon amie qui connaissait l'anglais de me l'expli-

36

quer. Elle me raconta de telles histoires! Les journaux étaient pleins de nouvelles sur son arrivée, ses sermons. On l'appelait 'l'apôtre de la paix'. C'est un Sage de l'Orient, disait mon amie, mais mon coeur me disait qu'il était beaucoup plus que ça. Qui était-il? Je n'aurais pas pu le dire. La tante de mon amie connaissait quelqu'un dont il avait guéri l'enfant. Il accomplissait des miracles. Oh, Beauchamps, j'avais besoin d'un miracle. Ça faisait trois ans que nous étions mariés et toujours pas d'enfant. Mes larmes, mes neuvaines, les cierges . . . ça ne servait à rien. Je priai, 'Mère du Ciel, laisse-moi le voir.'

Ce fut assez facile de trouver l'Hôtel Windsor. Une foule s'était assemblée et j'étais un peu à l'écart, anonyme, pas nerveuse mais tremblante d'excitation, me sentant pauvrement vêtue et hors de mon élément parmi ces gens élégants, parmi les anglais. Mais quand il est arrivé, je ne sentis plus de dépaysement, seulement un profond respect et beaucoup d'amour car, Beauchamps, il rayonnait d'une si belle lumière. Il avait le visage d'un saint, avec tout le bonheur du ciel et tous les fardeaux de la terre. Personne ne m'a vue quand j'ai fait le signe de la croix en sa sainte présence.

Puis, j'ai ressenti une grande honte lorsque je le vis, souriant, se promener parmi les gens et les saluer, car ils étaient comme des enfants, chacun désirant l'attention de son père, patient et fatigué, chacun désirant une solution à ses problèmes, une réponse à ses questions, à ses besoins, tout comme moi. J'ai voulu m'en aller mais je n'ai pas pu me détourner de sa silhouette rayonnante. Je me dis: 'Il ne connaîtra pas de repos. On le crucifiera avec nos questions. Nous voulons tous prendre de lui mais qui l'aidera dans sa grande oeuvre? Que Dieu le fortifie,' priai-je en silence.

A ce moment, comme si je l'avais appelé, il tourna son regard dans ma direction et, pour la première fois, j'en ressenti toute la force. Il n'y a pas de mots pour décrire cela, mon Jean-Paul, mais c'était comme s'il avait lu toutes les pages de mon âme. Mon coeur, qui battait avec fureur, fut soudain envahi par une paix que je n'avais jamais connue. Il y avait dans son regard triste toute la sagesse et la tendresse qu'on avait dû voir sur le visage de notre Seigneur. Il y avait une question aussi, mais je ne la comprenais pas. Ce moment me sembla éternel.

Puis il sourit et se détourna afin de répondre à quelqu'un qui lui avait adressé la parole et je sus ce que j'allais faire. Je devais le toucher, légèrement toucher son manteau. Je ne sais toujours pas si ce fut le courage ou la folie qui m'a poussée mais je n'ai pu résister à cette impulsion.

Inaperçue, je fis mon chemin dans la foule. Qui m'aurait remarquée quand il y avait ce saint homme parmi eux! Je m'approchai de plus en plus jusqu'à ce que je puisse presque le toucher. Alors la femme qui était devant moi et qui lui parlait se mit à pleurer doucement et, en se détournant, se déplaça de côté, me mettant face à face avec lui. Sans penser à ce que je faisais, j'ai fait une génuflexion pour toucher le bas de son manteau avec mes lèvres mais il me prit par le bras et me releva tout en retenant mon regard. Mes deux mains étaient dans les siennes. Je ne sais pas dans quelle langue il parlait mais je compris ses douces paroles: 'Non, ma fille.' Prestement, il sortit quelque chose de sa poche et le mit dans le creux de ma main avec un sourire amusé. Il me quitta sans dire un mot et s'éloigna si doucement que ma petite indiscrétion ne fut guère remarquée et ne causa pas d'embarras.

Je me suis alors effacée reculant lentement dans la foule, trop heureuse de s'avancer pour me remplacer. Puis je me suis mis à courir, traversant la place et m'arrêtant sous les arbres, pour reprendre mon souffle et continuer à regarder pendant quelques minutes, jusqu'à ce qu'il entre dans l'hôtel et que la foule se dissipe. Ce n'est qu'à ce moment que je me rappelai le cadeau qu'il avait placé dans ma main et que je tenais toujours serré entre mes doigts. Il y avait là deux petits bonbons. Je ne doutai pas à quoi ils devaient servir. Ce soir-là, Jean-Paul, ils allaient être notre banquet.

Quand j'ai conçu Pierre, je fus tenté de te le dire, mais comment aurais-je trouvé les mots? Et puis vinrent les autres enfants et il n'y eut plus de raison pour en parler car la vie continuait comme d'habitude. Je fus si heureuse de donner Pierre et Martine à l'Eglise que j'aurais aussi accepté volontiers de voir les autres prendre les Ordres s'ils avaient eu l'appel. Donc, je ne t'ai jamais parlé de ça, mon Beauchamps. Est-ce que tu souris au ciel quand tu me vois chaque année, le même jour, venir ici afin de rendre grâce?

Parfois je pense que les petits-enfants pourraient comprendre si je leur en parlais, surtout Céleste, qui est comme un ange de Dieu.

Peut-être je lui en parlerai un jour et l'amènerai avec moi. Je serais contente d'avoir sa compagnie dans l'autobus. On pourrait s'asseoir sous les arbres de la place, j'essayerais de le lui décrire. Mais qu'est-ce que je dirais si elle me demandait ce qu'il est advenu de l'Apôtre de la Paix car je ne l'ai plus jamais revu, ni n'ai entendu parler de son oeuvre. Mais je sais que c'était l'oeuvre de Dieu et qu'elle n'est pas perdue même après un demi-siècle.

Est-ce que Céleste rirait du pèlerinage d'une stupide vieille femme? Non, elle essayerait de comprendre. Elle est comme moi mais plus animée, plus curieuse et elle ne trouve pas de réponse dans l'Eglise. Elle lit sur Bouddha ou Mahomet, des sujets dont on ne parlait pas dans mon temps. Non, Céleste ne se moquera pas de l'oeuvre mystérieuse des Cieux.

traduit par Michael Power

SOME SORT OF FOREIGNER

Who shall say how much or how little of the Message given by [‘Abdu'l-Bahá] was understood by those persons, well-known and unknown, gentle and simple, who sought His presence in those days [in London] . . . It is not ours to know how many were conscious of the vital breath of love and wisdom and power, which was always around the Master, more penetrating and significant than even His words . . . Some were awed and transformed. Their very souls seemed wrapt by an unforgettable experience.

Sara Louisa, Lady Blomfield
The Chosen Highway

London
September 1911

I'm ever so glad you popped in, luv. Just sit yourself down and I'll be with you in 'alf a mo. When I finish basting the 'am we'll have a nice cuppa. The kettle'll soon be on the boil. I'm about to do a spot of baking so never mind the mess. Look at those apples, would you,

Maude! The best old Mattie the greengrocer 'ad, but they look like they died of a bad fright. And it isn't as if I didn't pay an arm and a leg for 'em. But they'll bake up nice in a tart, and Bill doesn't 'alf like a sweet, especially a good apple tart. I want to give 'im a bit of a treat tonight.

Y'know, 'e's a good man, my old Bill. Even though I grumble about 'im I really do appreciate my old geezer and I was thinking today, well, you silly old cow, you should show 'im, wouldn't 'urt a bit to show 'im. You get to taking one another for granted in a marriage over the years, I was thinking to meself, and you shouldn't be always 'aving a go at 'im.

Eow, I don't 'alf guess the neighbourhood from 'ere to Wapping 'ears us shouting at one another now and again, and I'm never shy about letting the old man know 'is faults, but it's all an 'abit of speech, like, a part of daily living, and not to be took too serious.

Not that 'e doesn't put me off; 'e 'as 'is aggravating ways, all right, but 'e's a decent sort— a good father and an 'ard worker. I've always said there's more to my Bill than a liking for a pint and a quick turn under the blanket. And 'e's smart, 'e is. I mean to say, like, 'im being in 'is trade, 'e gets to see all kinds, and from the inside out, so to speak. The 'igh and the low alike. So there's no use anybody putting on la-di-da airs with 'im, for 'e's seen 'em all in their knickers and with their 'air down, in a manner of speaking. So it isn't every day 'e's impressed.

Like yesterday, for instance, 'e comes in just as I laid the tea, but instead of tucking in as usual, 'e just sits there 'ardly speaking, so I'm thinking to meself, wot's 'e on about, and I says to 'im, is everything all right, luv?

Well, 'e doesn't 'alf give me a start when 'e says in a kind of funny, quiet voice so's I know 'e's been thinking it over, like —Gladdie, 'e says, do you suppose there's anything in this business of religion?

So I think for a moment, wot's 'e been up to? and I answer, casual like, well, there's some wot makes a right to-do about it; what do *you* think?

And 'e tells me 'e was on a job up in some posh place where Lady Whatzit-Thing-me lives and that the 'ouse was all in an uproar on account of 'er ladyship 'ad some very important guest—some sort of foreigner, but a real gentleman and a kind of preacher— and the place was buzzing with callers and everybody making a fuss over 'im, including 'er ladyship. She was a nice motherly sort, says Bill, but she'd let it be known it would be appreciated if 'e would get the work done and clear out smartly.

So 'e does 'is work quick, all right, and in such a tearing 'urry that 'e's nipped out and is 'alf-way down the block before 'e notices 'e's forgot 'is tools. Well, that's my Bill, I thinks to meself; 'is daydreaming doesn't 'alf drive me mad as you well know, Maude. So back 'e goes on the quick and gets 'imself let into the front passage, but before 'e knows wot's 'appening a door bursts open and a crowd of people comes into the passage and there's poor old Bill caught in the act and 'im wishing the floor would open up and swallow 'im, 'e was that confused.

Isn't that the limit! I says to 'im, wondering why 'e's not laughing fit to bust, because it's the kind of daft thing wot would tickle 'im, after it was over, and 'im not being one that'd be afraid to say Bob's-your-Uncle to the Archbishop of Canterbury if 'e 'ad a mind to.

So wot did you do? I says. Well, says Bill, I just stood there because the foreign gentleman was in the middle of the crowd and the minute 'e spots me 'e steps forward and the others step back, like, and 'e comes right over smiling like 'e knew me all my life, and 'e shakes me 'and and says *Welcome! Welcome!* I never met anyone like 'im 'e was that polite and friendly, says Bill.

So 'e speaks English? I says. I thought you said 'e was some sort of foreigner.

Eow, 'e was dressed foreign-like, says Bill, but 'e spoke English and it sounded all right to me.

Well, I guess there's foreigners and foreigners, Maude. Y'see, 'e was ever so nice to Bill, courteous like, asking 'im questions about where 'e lived and did 'e have a family.

I was thinking, wot a cheek! But Bill says it was like being asked by an old friend wot you 'adn't seen in a long time, and there was my Bill— you know 'ow 'e is with strangers, Maude; 'e uses words like they cost a pound apiece— there 'e was telling 'im about our Tom and Ellen and about me needing an operation and all— I'd 'ave died if

I'd known, 'im being a perfect stranger—and the old foreign gentleman says something like, I'll pray for your wife and *you* must pray, too. I daresay Bill was 'oping 'e'd leave off. My Bill praying, can you see it!

So Bill gets embarrassed and tells 'im that 'e doesn't know much about religious things, being as 'ow 'e's 'ad to work so 'ard all 'is life and no time for that—but 'e says it not cheeky, mind, with respect. Bill says there was something ever so nice about 'im; you could never be rude, like.

And the old man didn't 'alf surprise Bill by saying with a big smile and 'is voice booming all over the passage, *Good! Very Good!* And 'e goes on to say that work is a kind of prayer, too, and that if a man goes to work—well, like, to support 'is family or to help other people, it's like God understands 'e's busy and that's 'ow a working man prays, so to speak. Like, it's the reason wot counts with the Lord.

Well, if that didn't 'alf give my Bill something to think about! I'll tell you! It's funny, Maude, 'ow we never thought of it before, but when you stop to think, it makes good sense.

So then the gentleman says goodbye to Bill and wishes 'im good luck and all, and when somebody asks a question of the old man, Bill's able to slip away. And off 'e goes to work this morning, does Bill, whistling the place down and marching around like 'e was the Maharajah of Mile End. Eow, 'e's not going to forget that foreign gentlemen in an 'urry, mark my words!

So there 'e sat last night, see, letting 'is tea get cold and asking me in a daft voice, like wot I told you, did I think there was anything in religion. Him wot isn't exactly your plaster saint and wouldn't set foot in a church but for weddings and funerals.

Well, says I, I guess there's a lot of good people in the world and the Good Lord knows who they are if anybody does; and I don't reckon all of 'em do their praying in church, luv.

Eow, 'e's not a bad sort, my old Bill.

CRIMINAL MAESTRO

(Eduardo Duarte Vieira—First African Bahá'í Martyr)

Di, Duarte Vieira, di, se ruega,
¿Qué crimen te ganó tu celda?

Dejas testamento en lata trazado.
¿Cual fue, Duarte Vieira, tu pecado?

¿Cuándo y dónde has desviado,
Tal que el Cielo te ha alabado?

¿Qué delito has cometido?
Di, que sea por nosotros repetido.

Revela tu secreto; por ello
Ganamos nosotros también el Cielo.

Temores furtivos por ti sosegados,
Buscamos crímenes tan recompensados.

Enterrado ya el felón de Bahá
Bendice todo África.

¿Di, Duarte Vieira, di, se ruega,
Por qué crimen se te encarcela?

translated by Barbara Barrett

PART TWO:

SONGS AND SONNETS

Shall I write
And not of Thee through Whom my fingers bend
To hold my quill?

George Herbert
1593–1633

We read religious poems not to learn about
God but to learn about men.

Randall Jarrell
Poetry and the Age

SONG FOR A SORCERER

Some of His [Bahá'u'lláh's] enemies have even written poems about Him, which though intended for satire and sarcastic allusion, have in reality been praise. For instance a certain poet opposed to His Cause has said 'Beware! Beware! lest ye approach this person; for he . . . is a sorcerer. He charms men, he drugs them; he is a hypnotizer. Beware! Beware! lest you read his book, follow his example and associate with his companions because they are are the possessors of tremendous power and they are misleaders.'

'Abdu'l-Bahá

Beware, unwary hearts, beware,
For Satan sets enticing snare
And foul his kiss though seeming fair.

His sugared words mask poisoned plea
Inciting fools to perfidy.
Boundless, this vile sorcery.

Hypnotic charm and drugging spell
Advance the course of evil well;
He lures men to the bowels of hell,

Subdues the hapless with a glance
And pipes the heedless in wild dance.
Damned, the wretches he enchants.

For madness these will overtake
To quaff a wine which does not slake,
Doff head or turban for love's sake.

The unloosed sweetness of his song
Seduces souls to greatest wrong.
Oh strong the sway of Satan, strong.

The guileless who seek paradise
Are drowned in his inveigling eyes.
Who flout the ravisher are wise.

Shun his alluring, languorous look,
Spurn the treachery of his book;
When his pen shrilled all heaven shook.

Avoid the ember lest it flare,
Flee the hawk as would the hare.
Beware, unwitting ones, beware.

TRYST

As bidden I waited expectant on the hill of faithfulness, yet inhaled not from them that dwell on earth the fragrance of fidelity.

Bahá'u'lláh

What more is asked, my love; what more than this
Charmed hour on your couch? Did I not dance
In silver sandals for you, my entreating glance
Soliciting your warm approving kiss?
For you I brought the hyacinth, oiled my hair—
Were it courtly art you asked, I have not failed.
Did I not approach your tent in mauve dusk, veiled
And scented, demure in paint? Beloved, there
By your pillow is my gemmed ring
As if forgotten—a baubled oath! Hold
It to your lips, by kiss assay the gold;
I would have it pledge my swift returning.
I leave . . . Yet more is asked? O lover, speak!
Your eyes hold tears! You sadly stroke my cheek!

SHELTER

for Geoffrey Nash

Love does not give at first the frescoed room
richly arrased, low fire in the grate,
sumptuous carpets from some fabled loom,
sensuous pillows, beside the gilt swan-bed
a silver bowl of asters, fruit-heaped plate.
Love yields not soon a banquet ready-spread,
with brimming cup and lute song. Do not assume
warm welcoming kiss and handclasp await
love's early guest, gauche in that silent room,
dumb with wonder, faint of heart with dread.
Love offers first the suppliant at its gate
faith's bricks and planks and rusted nails that wound.
To fragile shelter built to love's spare plan,
gold-laden, comes royal lover's caravan.

THE SONG OF <u>KH</u>ADÍJIH-BAGUM

O well-beloved! . . . Be patient in all that God hath ordained concerning the
Báb and His family.

The Báb addressing His wife in the
Qayyúmu'l-Asmá'

. . . a lone and noble woman who suffered in silence for forty years.

H. M. Balyuzí

All in green went my Love riding
My heart sank fully sore
To know the One Whose stirrup I kissed
I would see no more
no more
see Him Whom I adore.

To know Him clad in rope and chain
And hung above the throng
The world's One Light by evil quenched
And I be left but long
but long
left sorrow as my song.

All in green went my Love riding
His counsel my sole balm
Be patient under God's decree
This parting speeds the dawn
the dawn
speeds never-fading Dawn.

CRIMES

If it were in trespass that my head lay
Drowsing on Your breast I should choose that sin,
Court the penalty dear villainy might win
Nor ask parole, but love the fine I'd pay.
Were it a braver wrong to brush Your brow
Gently with felonious, panting kiss
I'd be confirmed to be recidivist
Pledging reform but swift to break the vow.
What grand offence may dwarf courage contract?
I'd seize upon this boldest transgression;
If deed were sweet no less would be confession
With Your forgiveness fitted to the act.
The forfeit as delightsome as the crime—
I'd be criminal and make Your justice mine!

THE JOURNEY

Go straight on then as thou hast been commanded.

Qur'án 11:114; 42:14

And they will warn you, children, as they stand
In wan ardour at the dense thicket's rim
That your pitch venture is folly, a dim
Dangerous progress over untracked land
Ambushed with bogs in which illusions mire,
Keen fang and talon glint from every tree
And murky bats career and lean wolves prey.
Reason is soon victim and then desire—
A sharp cry marks the kill no startled plea
Postpones. No one returns uncrazed, the cautious say,
And many perish. Who might guess
How few whose passion wins the sought caress.
Who counsel flight from Love's far lair are wise
But O! not they shall see the Lover's eyes.

ṬÁHIRIH'S SONG

I'd explain all my grief, dot by dot, point by point . . .

(from a poem usually attributed to Ṭáhirih)

Line by line, dot by dot,
I tell my tale:
Heart's grief the plot.

Dot by dot, line by line,
I weave the theme
Soul's hope makes mine.

Sob by sob, breath by breath,
I spell remoteness,
Know it death.

Sigh by sigh, moan by moan,
I mark One Presence
As my home.

Point by point, page by page,
I cite the bond
For which I rage.

Stroke by stroke, plea by plea,
My longing
The calligraphy.

Sweet the mystery *Váv* contains,
In Great Reversal
Joys wed pains.

Meaning teems in smallest part
When every '*Ayn*
Reveals the heart.

Skims the hand, fleet it strides,
Leaps wondrously,
Bahjí describes.

Dream-born words as might foretell
A bridal gown
And silent well.

Blood my ink, desire my quill,
The pen names Love
and awed grows still.

Peerless Name! Peerless Face!
My tears each line
And dot erase.

Cleanse the page of telling stains—
The Upright *Alif*
Yet remains.

IN LIEU OF PANEGYRIC

*To May Maxwell . . . Lua Getsinger . . . Martha Root . . . belong the
priceless honour of having conferred, through their services and sacrifice, a
lustre upon the American Bahá'í community for which its representatives
. . . may well feel eternally grateful.*

Shoghi Effendi
God Passes By

You did not need, great ladies, our pale praise
Who had in his all heaven's; who as you
Gaily stride the sky know our embarrassed cry
That angels should undo our timorous ways
To tend to miracles. We, mincing few
Tenants of a grey plain, whose nervous eye
Is peeled for tinselled honour will not trace,
Gasping, your pell-mell plunge from pride to grace.

O might that fall be ours! We clutch power
Like the wine-cruse; pellicle and dregs are sweet
To those who know no other wine. Strike from our hand
The sour brew, the perishable flower
From which the mind weaves garlands, the vain meat
Of will that does not nourish. Grant us to understand
The banquet you enjoy. From your pantheon
Unseat us from our thin feast to speed the dawn.

COSTUMES

Were we then too perilously earnest;
Too quick to wear a visible abasement,
A piety of fashion in degree as lent
Proof of our high purpose, not so as peers spurned us
But as slightly shamed their paler show?
Or did we copy slavishly their dress
In mind and manner, clothe in liberal clichés, confess
Ourselves concerned but not committed, and so
Secure a mirrored admiration of their worth,
Ourselves corrupting? Though privately there swarmed
Martyrs in our dreams, publicly we warmed
To tenets socially approved, and fled rebirth.

Who are these naked few in hobbling chain
Yet run lightfooted, laughing, robed in pain?

SONG OF THE CUP

Sweet wild words my true-love sang,
His sugared voice endearing.
Clear on the perfumed air it rang
But I was not for hearing.
    Gay was my song
    in the noisy throng
    and I was not for hearing.

White was the rose my true-love cast,
White as his hand which cast it,
I trod underfoot the bloom that lasts,
Disdainfully I danced past it.
    My laughter was loud
    in the whirling crowd,
    disdainfully I danced past it.

Tender the kiss my true-love blew,
Piercingly tinged with sorrow.
Deeming all hearts, like mine, untrue
I sought new lips each morrow.
    Swift in the dance
    I paid no glance
    And sought new lips each morrow.

Honeyed the cup my true-love gave
From grape unknown to men.
Who pause to taste will love enslave
And linger to taste again.
    Captive of wine
    From unslaking vine
    I linger to drink again.

INK

What is the ink with which I best could write
The covenant that's imaged by Your name
So one who finds me faint or failed exclaim,
This is his love! Would trace of lees invite
That recognition, or might blood proclaim
The louder Who held fast my heart in claim?

How shall I tell my love? It is not stone
That's ablest to endure time's levelling hand
Mindlessly erasing man's anguished tale.
Historians invent from knucklebone
Of lords and slaves bright brave legends and brand
Them true— but altering myths not long prevail.

Songs fade away; a poem's a fragile thing—
Were faith sure signature to name You King?

SILENCES

Before ultimate silence falls the song may stop.
Is it stridulous life's raving gibber
From which the singer shrinks, mute, aquiver
And aghast lest life's careless hand let drop
A weight of loud, bawling love upon his
Fastidious aloneness, the uncluttered stage
Of self-applauded postures of grief and rage?
If song were real life, then silence were failure. Is
It not true when you, as in my dreams,
Unloosed across my circling hands your hair
It was our silences that tears laid bare?
That quiet shouted down my songs and themes.
Then who might tell were song or silence meet
When songster sprawls at God's great listening feet?

DREAM SONG

Mother, hold me to your breast,
I saw the sun rise in the West,
A pauper raised and crowned in gold,
A noble exiled, homeless, cold,
A shepherd penning history,
A lover burning in the sea.

Mother, clasp me in your arms,
My heart grows faint with quaint alarms,
I saw a child who tutored priest,
A man who had his heart for feast,
A queen neglected in the dust,
Divines and Judges none would trust.

Dearest mother, comfort me,
I saw tears flow from every tree,
In crowded streets as if entranced
A living candelabrum danced,
I saw a fair bride couched alone
In silent well to drown in stone.

Mother, mother, hold my hand,
I saw gardens bloom in desert sand,
A singing man who had been dumb,
A bell that pealed without a tongue,
A witless scholar once well versed—
Whose Order yields a world reversed?

In dreams, the future seeks rehearsal.
Mark well the world's, the heart's reversal.

CHOICES

I gazed into the eyes of Shoghi Effendi and I knew the world was ashes.
William Sears

How gladly would I win my way with wit
Were heaven purchased for a clever jest
Or words held any meaning faced with it.
Gathering from my songs the cunning best
I would beguile the angels in their play
Ingratiate myself with this gay brief
And bright avowal of my finest day
Or sway them with recital of my grief.
I would counterfeit my prayer if it were coin
Relinquish love and part with sight or breath
Toil forever— mind, limb, heart and loin—
Choose these, my King, above this bloodless death.

Prepare the coward for this daunting deed.
Who calls and points the path knows pain the steed.

IT IS AN EASY THING TO LOVE THE DEAD

It is an easy thing to love the dead
Who have no power to hurt, who do not strive,
Cower, despair, feel guilt, nor hope, nor dread,
Nor wound by all such means they did alive
As telling, faithful mirrors of our need.
We then descry them fully compassed, real,
As fruit belies the dry, unlikely seed
Or as air's pungent proof its tang, its feel.
They are unarguable as roses,
Unanswerable as trees; the torn earth
And tortured sap forgot. None supposes
That pain and dung had fed this birth.

But I would have you live, my love, although
I die with every thrust by which you grow.

AN IRISH AIR

'Twas not some woman's yellow hair
Did carefree hearts of lads impair
As she might ease were they to kiss.
A Beauty passed exceeding this.

'Twas not the envy of a lass
Which drew each woman from her glass
To test her worth by suitor's whim.
A Lover passed. They followed Him.

'Twas not a young girl's laughing air
Which stopped the husband on the stair
To curse time's theft and death's rank haste.
A Cup was passed. He paused to taste.

'Twas not swords glinting in the sun
Which maddened every mother's son
To prove the valorous blood engaged.
They looked within where Battle raged.

'Twas not a minstrel's tinkling air
Which called the children from the fair
To caper gleefully in the street
That Life and Song should be so sweet.

'Twas not spring's leaf-scent on the breeze
Which drew the old priest from his knees
To wonder Whose light footfall brings
Such glad renewal to all things.

Through the half-light, towards the Dawn,
Whose gleaming sandal leads us on?
'Twas not some woman's yellow hair
Did lilting Irish hearts ensnare!

CAPRICCIO

The soul to the Insistent Self
Fierce courage doth display . . .
Thus sang the minstrel to the Court
When bade to sing and play.

Cease, jongleur! cried one stalwart Knight,
I've known a joust or two.
Sing now a gallant battle song.
  Quoth he: *I do, I do!*

The soul to the Insistent Self
Doth tenderness display . . .
Thus sang once more the wanderer
To all the Court's dismay.

Prithee desist! spake one wan maid,
My heart is hung with rue.
Wilt thou not sing of love betrayed?
  Quoth he: *I do, I do!*

GROOM'S SONG

. . . your days of horsemanship are yet to come.
                    Words of the Báb to Mullá Ḥusayn

        Why do you sit, sire,
        Astride your great roan?
        How came you here?
        Do you travel alone?

        On what do you gaze
        From the crest of the hill?
        Why muse so intently
        So silent and still?

Green is your mantle
And moonwhite your steed;
The set of your brow
Foretells a grave deed.

Are you a satrap,
A prince or a lord?
What is the wisdom
In your soft eyes stored?

Far less than a shadow
I'd count the world's worth
Were you the Master
I've sought since my birth.

Your beast paws and shivers;
Might this portend
The chaos and pain
Of the shallow world's end?

I've dreamed of you often
And woke with the thought
That truth does not die
By sword or by shot.

Lift me aloft, sire,
Your patient, strong roan
Or is yours a journey
You must make alone?

I would follow to heaven
On foot if I must
You charging before
Through bright arches of dust.

CORAL AND PEARLS
For Hilda and Morrie Phillips

*O my Lord, O my Lord! These two bright moons are wedded in Thy love
. . . He hath let loose the two seas, that they may meet each other: Between
them is a barrier which they overpass not . . . Make Thou this marriage to
bring forth coral and pearls.*

'Abdu'l-Bahá

Love, as I lean toward you and make my home
In your warm, whorled, listening receptivity
Where you admit my name as if it were your own,
Fear wisely that my weakness and soft moan
Ask licence to betray you to captivity
As moon to my sun. It is your unmingled light,
Inviolate, self-kindled and enhancing that might
Tempt my pride to snuff it, eclipse the inner white
Wonder my warrant forged in passion cannot own.
Teach me that not in trespass do I harvest more
Than your surging tenderness yields to my sight.
Bid me bless the barrier to your invasion
When our seas meet. Tide-cast wealth affords persuasion
That each sea must hold its moon, each touch its shore.

INSCRIPTION FOR THE HEAD OF A PIN

*To Persian mystics all writing emanates from a single calligraphic dot on the
page. The Báb is the Primal Point, 'from which have been generated all
created things.'*

Marzieh Gail

One dot:
From this
all else begot.

Take pains:
This sign
all else contains.

Grave well:
This mark
worlds will tell.

Eloquent pin!
One dot—
infinitude within.

SONG OF THE SYBIL
(after a fragment by Sappho)

Mother, I cannot mind my wheel
My fingers ache, my throat is dry.
I see all good nailed to a cross
In silhouette against the sky.

Husband, I cannot tend the loom
My heart grows faint, my sight grows dim.
I see all good as target given,
A thousand muskets aimed at him.

Daughter, I cannot leave the fire
My thin frame shakes, my blood runs cold.
I see all good cast in a pit
And decked with chains, but not of gold.

Grandchild, I cannot leave my bed
My life's breath fades, my vision blurs.
My soul draws onwards toward a voice:
Who loves all good, all good is hers.

LOVE STORY

A prince upon a milk-white steed
Flashed by my dazzled gaze
And though he merely glanced at me
I'll love him all my days.

> *Hush, child, you cannot know of love!*
> *Perhaps there passed a snowy dove . . .*

I glimpsed him sweeping past the door;
His are the lips I'd kiss.
I must arise and follow him
Though pain be cost of this.

> *By dream, perchance, you were beguiled*
> *Or by the passing wind, my child . . .*

I cast beneath his mount's great feet
The rose pinned to my waist;
My hands now wear a scarlet tint,
My breast is laid to waste.

> *Vain was my prayer to speed him past!*
> *My child, it was your heart you cast . . .*

Mother, will you heal this wound
With fragrant herb and balm,
Or must I sink and never kiss
That face I dote upon?

> *No reprieve will unguent give;*
> *You'll die, my child, and dying, live.*
> *How well I know love's course is wild—*
> *Regard my shattered breast, my child!*

PART THREE:

THE MILK, THE HONEY—Poems from Israel

The mausoleum of the Báb . . . 'the spot round which the Concourse on high circle in adoration' . . . nestling in the heart of Carmel, the 'Vineyard of God'; flanked by the Cave of Elijah on the west, and by the hills of Galilee on the east; backed by the plain of Sharon, and facing the silver-city of 'Akká, and beyond it the Most Holy Tomb [of Bahá'u'lláh], the Heart and Qiblih of the Bahá'í world . . .

Shoghi Effendi

Or is't so, as some green heads say,
That now all miracles must cease . . .?

Henry Vaughan
1622–1695

SONG FOR THE WAITING STONES

Take me with the Jerusalem stone, place me in the walls . . . my pining
hopes will sing toward the Messiah's advent.

Yehuda Karni
1884–1948

Spurned, he huddles chilled, beyond the wall
and eats dry crust and makes his little fire;
mends a worn sandal and attends his lyre;
sees darkness gather, sees the low flames fall.
Inchoate voices carry on the air.
He hears one sadly speak of long-dead kings.
One calls out in rage, and one in love; there,
sorrowed but uncontrite, another sings.
The stiffnecked city keeps its ancient ways,
quibbles, quarrels, counts gold, seals its proud gates,
retails desire, laughs, fills grudgeful days,
despairs of the delivery it awaits.
The faithful minstrel bides, though long and long,
who received, will ravish stones with honeyed song.

PILGRIM SONG

Swift would I be, Lord, swift; on dancing feet
Hastening would come, if called, nor brook delay,
Gleefully come— though lone the perilous way
And stern and starless— still would my step be fleet;
And singing would come and, with song, entreat
Angels to chart my path. Though Thou might slay
Me, still would I come and rejoicing stay
Quick or faint or slain at Thy welcoming feet.

Gifts would I bring— choice, my gifts, and many—
Laden with gifts, and laughing, would I come;
Or pauperized come— hands cupped, bereft of any
But hoarded hot tears— to stand before Thee, dumb.
Swift would I be, Lord, if Thou wouldst but call—
My aim, my hope, my home, my love, my all.

THOUGHTS ON BLINDNESS

*As a pilgrim, I think it must be heaven to live in the Holy Land. Or do you
find it necessary, in order to accomplish the work you were brought here to
do, to blind yourself against a recognition of the reality of where you are?*
Letter from a pilgrim

If this were heaven and I its svelte tenant
why should the hill studded with sullen stones
affront me with its putative history
and I stand exiled and uncomprehending
before the avowal of its flaunted cypress
in grim denial of the shy flowered evidence
of the hostile prickly pear?

No manna falls as I walk amid the marble edifices
which hold inaccessible mysteries
and ordinary dust. Mark how the paths are flanked
by unendearing domestic orange trees,
the obtuseness of pedestrian geranium.
What is here save that with which
we lavishly invest it?

Shall I call this heaven when I too must beg
Do not abandon me, my best Beloved;
revere as Zion this incomprehensibly storied waste
which does not support the lilac
or offer against fatigue the sharp
emerald surprise of the glacial lake?
How might I love a land to which
my Love was led in chains?

Only with the fading of the machine's necessary clatter
do I see the swooning figures with averted eyes
circumambulate the Crimson Ark,
hear distant but insistent
the Voice of the Crier,
the Ruler's awesome tread.

Now dare I welcome the timid surmise
that my keyboard's urgent multiloquence
resounds in Mecca,
shakes hearts in Rome?

A PARABLE FOR THE WRONG PEOPLE
for David Hofman

*You know it says in the Bible that things are said in parables so that the
wrong people won't understand them and so get saved . . .*

Robert Frost
The Figure a Poem Makes

Noah will say this journey is definitely not
for the timid and the overwrought;
will warn that you must embark upon the voyage
with the utmost care, consider the destination,
ask the arresting question: Does passion lead me there?
Parables today are not in fashion
but let us say, for argument's sake, you choose to go by sea
and— if you will bear with me— we might allude
to the goal as being (don't anticipate!)
not Atlantis or Utopia, but *Certitude*
(to suggest a tone of hazard and imply
there's more at stake than just a change of air.)
Right, then. Noah is consulted— a reliable chap,
a long time in the business, can read a map,
know's what's best to wear, and why,
and covenants— as these things go— a reasonable fare.

Noah's said to be a character, a salty card,
one who doesn't hold with mincing words.
Straight-out he'll tell you to disregard
the Tourist Bureau's convincing spiel—
he'll say that's for the birds.
He dismisses the cheerful pamphlet that offers faith
like a glossy travel-folder's package deal—
(see the technicolour page slide open to reveal
the sun-drenched island of delectable appeal!)
The Bureau lied, says Noah. It puts him in a rage
to suggest the sum of virtues may be toured for education
by the polite and grinning liberal in need of tonic,
inoculated intellectually (hear the squeamish squeal!)
against such primitive, unhygienic perils as chronic
and committed rapture, or incipient dedication.
Where d'ya think you're going, Noah's been known to ask,
on a vacation? In addition,
he's been heard to take to task,
in terms offensive to a purist, the
pursy clench-jawed tourist, bent grimly on attrition,
who seeks a self-inflicted martyrdom— dutiful,
highly prized, unbeautiful— self righteousness thus canonized.
THIS martyrdom, when all that died was joy?
Let's have some authenticity! Smile, there, boy!
(Oh, best shape up or leave the ship when Noah speaks;
note well the colour rising in his cheeks!)

Forget all notions of a luxury cruise. *The Ocean's*
larger than the ship, warns Noah, *the passengers are many,*
and untrained and various the crew. He'll tell you
of the lean provision of devotion, of nefarious mutiny,
the wild and mounting waters, the weeks and
months of never-ending dark. *A deluge, folks,*
is not a lark, he'll gruffly roar. And liking to embellish
his own jokes he'll add with relish:

All ashore that's going ashore! He's often heard to mutter
some homespun maxim—'*A ship and the faint-hearted
are soon parted*' or '*The vulgar truth, m'lads, may seem uncouth*'
—(laughing uproariously, of course, for his appreciation
of his wit is utter. But mark the scowl designed to wither
those inclined to dally or to dither.)

Noah will say this journey is definitely not
for the timid and the overwrought;
not for the vainly pious,
the pusillanimous of spirit,
the bloodless prig. This much is plain:
not for those wary and in despair of love,
this ardent voyage on the unvariable storm-lashed brig,
the unreasonable rain,
the long wait for the salient dove
to bring the living twig.

NOTES ON EROSION
for Peter Moore

Do not doubt that love renews itself
under the cool, metallic stars,
springs up intractably
like the pesky weed
to outrage our stark order,
and being lopped or trampled
yields its head but not its root
which feeds insatiably
in the heart's thin soil.

Denied, love then rapaciously
makes its season in our fevered dreams
from which we wake aghast
the taste of wet leaves on the tongue,
astute voracious tendrils at the throat,
our trembling palms gummy
with mould and knowledge.

Love does not die with blighted hope
nor Spring's frail harvest of desire;
it does not fail before the
mind's accusing noon-bright stare
nor wither under reason's chastening ice.
Neglect will foster, and dismay
but fertilize its thrusting growth.

Oh do not doubt that love
thrives in the desert
where the resolute verbena
unarrestably insinuates itself
through the socket of despair's bleached skull.

Let us, then, admit the ravishing vine,
astonish Death
with our fierce festoons,
with our green and wily succulence.

PRAYER FOR THE TRUE BELIEVER

God, do not rob us of our authentic Magdalene,—
for the prurient, to meet their obscene, implacable necessity,
will recreate her false, vile,
vitreous-eyed, lips overpainted by vacuity,
annul her smile,

etch her face with acid
distilled of their own bile,
place in her unwitting mouth—
as ready for the pomegranate's lush
red goodness as for the lemon's stinging tart—
their own disclaimed and shameless words,
assign to her the darkest works
with which their dreams are furnished;
induce in her dementia, replace her heart
with a sullen, evil engine exhumed
in secret from their listless hearts'
atrophied veins;
clothe her lewdly, slut's bangle at her wrist,
and set her in the market, bizarrely perfumed,
to atrociously vituperate the innocent and
beguile the fool. She would tell—
this deranged and wanton puppet—
their whorish lies, corrupt plain-dealing,
pervert our commonality,
pollute our well,
distort the poem
and put an end to music.
She would mate with the unspeakable beast and
call it love— her mutant spawn would overrun the city.
One terrible midnight she would stealthily arise
and, enacting their ambition,
overturn the hushed and holy Temple,
profane the sacred garden
where the true Mary lies.

O give us, Lord, in every age, Thy Magdalene— the true.
She must not die, for with her dies
repentance and communion— would this be meet?
Dead, what should be known of unconsidered tears
and who might know Thee risen?
Who anoint Thy feet?

SIGHTSEEING

Ḥusayn, a son of 'Abdu'l-Bahá, was born in 1888 and died in his eighth year. An adventurous child, he liked to explore his surroundings and when asked where he had been would say he had been sightseeing (Tamáshá) but mispronouncing it Tabáshá in his childish way. In the Tablet Bahá'u'lláh revealed at the boy's passing He incorporated the mispronounced word saying, in effect, that in the realms of God the child was now 'sightseeing'. This excerpt from the Tablet has been engraved on the headstone of Ḥusayn in the Muslim cemetery in 'Akká where many of the believers mentioned in Memorials of the Faithful *are entombed.*

The will caulks against invasion
by that liquid rushing world which unbidden
overwhelms the brief and hard-won equilibrium
where the heart's frail craft coasts welcomely unperturbed,
braced to deflect the dips and swings
threatening to capsize it in unforeseen eddies
or fling it uncontrolled to perilous brinks.

The Thresholds today will be avoided,
with their treacherous accepting silence
which refuses to be adversary to the disarmed self
forcing thus a meaningless esthetic quarrel.
Not today will the eye ferry to renewal
on the pilgrims' wonder, nor find its own,
nor wince at the candle misaligned
narrowing to justify the self-imposed expulsion
by fixing rebelliously on the carpet's grating flaw,
its design suddenly vulgar and inadequate.
Look how the docile petals lie, already curling.
One would not have chosen this, not any of it,
that vase, that rug,
the wringing of the spirit, the remorse,

this very room at once too simple and ornate
too human and divine
and ultimately right. Ultimately, too, a matter of indifference.
Let concentration on the birdcall and the dustmotes
arrest the inundation of
What place is this? and *Who am I?*
the veering towards the open wet beyond.

In armistice with amazement, mere sightseer,
I spend the day with pilgrims,
safely distanced from the tumultuous rapids
they traverse gratefully in their nine-day greed,
the detached host facilitating their heartswum passage
but am undone to sink with them in 'Akká
at the graveside of the child Ḥusayn
defenceless before the ambush of the headstone,
divinity drenching deeper for this humanness.

Here *Tábashá*
in a storm of tenderness
sweeps me out to lashing seas
where beyond all buoys,
in full consent,
I drown.

TIKKUN HAZOT
—for Ya'akov and Chaya—

Tikkun Hazot *(an act of mending). This midnight watch of the pious Jews in which they mourned the destruction of the temple and the dispersion of the people was, in Hebrew legend, the possible moment of miracle. The King Messiah, it was thought, would enter Jerusalem through the* Shaar Harahamim, *the Mercy Gate, in the old wall of the city.*

And should you come, deliverer,
will the Knesset heed,
the lusty hawkers put aside their wares and
disputations to seize the palm and dance
with the bankers and the children, and the
youthful lovers blissfully neglectful
on the poppied slope?
Might this be the midnight watch
larded with miracles
for which the pious shiverer
faint with despair and ardent supplication
petitions the numb unanswering air?

We feed our cogent dream with candles
straining for a sign. O breathe on us!
The dumb dust will rise and sing
beneath your sandals. Regard us, then,
and the stone stairs
worn by our expectant feet. Glance
toward the wall cemented with
our covenanted hope.
Do our piteous upraised hands not speed
our rescue? Come! In mercy, come! Surprise
our gate, redeemer, where
our stricken daughters wait
with streaming eyes
and hear no laughter from our silent sons.

Chooser, choose this moment—
for if our ritual and righteousness not bring you,
might our need?

THE VISITORS

Among those who visit . . . some were recalled to life . . . But others, in truth, have simply passed through; they have only taken a tour.

'Abdu'l-Bahá

Visitors to the Shrine of the Báb are requested as a mark of respect to remove their shoes before entering.

Israel Guide Book

With the punctuality of doubt the visitors arrive
and comply with the quaint instruction, giggling or in awe,
then falter by the door which parts with the irresistible certainty
of insight to draw them forward. Death might be like this,
subduing, mysteriously familiar, exquisitely on-drawing, and
no less distant than the perfumed Threshold toward which they
move as to reunion or their execution. Has there come one
who faints for milk and honey? One who panted on his pillow
for the fabulous unchanging Friend? They pad from sight.
Is this for some the rapt and bided moment?

Along the colonnade the efficient shoes are strewn
in blatant promiscuity or drawn apart chastely in fastidious
reprimand—but all a jumble of inverted decapitation—
to stab us with the poignancy of absence,
the marble's remote cool invitation to a higher competence
dearer, grown concentrate by this flawing human detritus.
It is as though all who entered were decanted
leaving a sediment to shout of identity in the still garden
where the inoffensive trees shrink deeply in anonymity
and the geraniums, raucously red, are mute, and even
the flighty birds, given so to gossip and impertinence,
open their throats in orison or celebratory song.

Is it our shoes which lend us arrogance and all authority?
Soled in callous leather we stomp wilfully to power,
run rough-shod and reckless to ill-chosen destinations,
teeter to hysteria and loss on highest heels,
and to love skip or scuff, humbled beggars on naked skin.
Even unoccupied and in democratic disarray
the shoes tell of solidity and purpose.
The surrounding space is vague with blank light
like the faces of children waking from the mutiny of dreams
when the faintest flicker of their eyelashes
might cleave us with tenderness.
Here in all the lapping greenness nothing but the Edifice
is seen as white.

Inside, some will cost the carpet and the chandelier
wonder when the show begins and turn in disappointment
from the musk-breathed silence to regain the acute reality
of postcards and the tour-guide's hearty dissertation.
But some shedding more than their leather weight might stay
ballooning with elation in the hushed throb of all that quiet
to evaporate, be so transfigured as never to touch earth again,
and all the practical shoes left waiting
contemptuous of such high-jinks
will yawn and tap impatiently a while
and then clatter away to board the tour bus briskly and regale
the gawping passengers with an amazing tale.

THE TROUBLE WITH MOUNTAINS

We come to this mountain late
in laggard wonder
and atrophied awe,
in distrust of the prompting of angels,
the voice in the thunder.

Like the old plainsman brought dazed
to the coast to die,
needing to hate
Vancouver and his death
who glared sullenly at its peaks
which to outwit defeat
he'd never try
protesting they block the view
and stifle breath.

An ant's dusty truth. We gaze
at our thorn-stabbed festering feet.
It is too late, too late,
the bruising stones reveal
to follow to the summit
One Whose feet were steel.

And do not hear the battered bird
high in the torturing wind: *Pass! Pass!*
With adamant soul
and sharpest sight
on feet of brass!

THE DYNAMICS OF EDEN

Know that nothing which exists remains in a state of repose . . . all things are in motion . . . Movement is necessary to existence, which is either growing or declining.

'Abdu'l-Bahá

All that Eden offered now is mine,
a well-selected wife and modest powers
not abused or vaunted, companionship
in honoured standing, full use of my hours
and rectitude. My several selves came one in time.

To hold this perfect balance what need I do
but dodge droll dislodging miracles, tread
warily past tempters, give love the slip
and apples ample berth, strike ambition dead,
and folly— in vain embrace the static lie as true?

A SUDDEN MUSIC

The world is sudden music, and I dance . . .

Horace Holley 'The Dance'
from *Divinations and Creation*

A taint of preening calculation
makes of our knowledge knowingness,
carries us too soon from innocence
and exaltation. Do we give offence
with our borrowed and embellished
choreography of reverence?

Under politely peevish interrogation
the pilgrim child,
her eyes ashine,
without pretence
announces that alone
within the Master's Shrine
she prayed, and feeling happy stayed
and broke into dance rapturously—
(does she observe our anxious adult glance?)
— *I had nothing else to give Him* . . .
and exulting floats away, fulfilled,
a rush of swirling skirt
and evanescence.

We, deft practitioners
of protocols of piety
are stranded on uncertainty
who had entered and then left
that rare Presence,
rehearsed petitioners,
joylessly
and empty-handed.

THE REPLENISHMENT OF WONDER

Commemoration of the Ascension of Bahá'u'lláh: Bahjí, May 29
1:45 a.m.

What is here that might replenish wonder
Wheedle the taut fact-infatuated mind
From service to the acrobatic will?
Does hope revive on pebbled paths under
The false moons of lamps or the slack heart find
Renewal fostered in this scented shadowed still?

The dreaming figures weave as in a dance,
Silently adoring or embalmed in awe
Only of their ritual of reverence.
Not in patterns of worshipful trance
But beyond the tall blue-painted door thaw
Releases us to marvel.
                    Let it commence:
The lamplit room, the snowy pallet. Now
Amaze at the meek petal-cradling slippers, how
Unprotesting, in caressing warmth, they shod
The iron feet that bore the weight of God.

TO PRAISE

If it were praise to call aloud Your name
in the gentle dawn, the proud and whirling noon
and tearfully at midnight, the callous moon
looking on, then have I praised, and will again,
        if this were praise.

If it were praise to fix in the cool still
centre of being Your imaged essence
till need fed on a notion of Your presence,
then have I praised and yet again I will,
        if this were praise.

If it were praise to be slain by You, not
with the bold scarlet witness of spilled blood
but that quiet drowing in the heart's own flood
by which this world's subdued, the other's bought—
        if this were praise, O!
        strike the amazing blow!

EDEN, AND ALL THAT
For Käthe and Guy Murchie

[*Knowledge*] *is earthly of the mind,*
But Wisdom heavenly of the soul.

Alfred Tennyson
In Memoriam cxiii

In truth I was bored
in the genial garden,
longed for something more ribald
than my tranquil lot
(I, the one-rib wonder)
and found Adam damnably dull,
excessively affable and mild.
And besides, he snored. I thought:
how dreary to be incapable of blunder!

All that endless innocence
was terribly wearing
and the chatter of the animals
quite drove me wild.
Just what *do* you say
to an amiable elephant, or a gruff? Tearing
around in the buff—
a decorous pastime this, and no disgrace—
did not for long amuse.
I tired of bland witlessness. Enough!
I dreamed of choices,
fancied high-heeled shoes,
a touch of lace and other voices.
So I began to plot. What had I
to lose save choicelessness?
Too much euphoric contentment
can give a girl the blues for
virtue unexercised smells of rot.

I imagined another arrangement,
conceived how I might conceive a child.
Adam (I told myself to justify my plan)
might like a son or several. So then
I talked it over with The Man.
You found the courage after all, he grinned.
We'll call the game 'The Fall'. Of course
You'll bear the blame, they'll say you sinned
when the story's told. I have my reputation
to uphold, after all, so you're the one.
Go to it girl, let's start the fun.

Persuading the stupid snake
to play bent tempter didn't take
much doing—I owed it to the legend—and
he, like Adam, wasn't very bright.
Once I'd lured my husband to the spot,
displayed the red and luscious sphere
and spoke of knowledge being power he
overcame his fear in that fraught hour
and was quick to take a bite.

That done, I knew the course was clear:
expulsion with fig leaves, and eternal shame.
The Man winked and I almost giggled
when Adam asked, *What have we done, my dear?*
but he didn't guess the game.
To calm him I looked coy and shyly pouted,
stuck out my curvaceous hips and wriggled
(I censor what he shouted) but then
Adam, unprotesting, made his first free choice;
the result was so arresting that
admittedly it caused me to rejoice.

The rest is known, of course,
but let me say
my scheme is still unfolding;
bear with me, girls, I'll have my way.
Meanwhile Adam, still a pompous bore
(but growing lovable
and ever eager for my kiss)
records the history woven from my myths,
and boasts and brags and plays at war
and doesn't know my plan to bring
a willed and chosen peace to all my sons,
in time, in time. That was my vow
in Eden. Not the lobotomized trance
of that pallid place but a greater thing.
I swear there'll be a silencing of guns;
I pledge new wine, new song, and dance.

As things seem now
I've not much improved my station
but I mark small gains
and patience is my strength.
I'll lead my children to elation
at length, my dears, at length,
as grain by grain a coast or
desert's moved. Ah, not for all
Adam's ribs or knowledge would I exchange
my thorny wisdom,
my spirit's luminous pains.

DRILL

Do men think when they say 'We believe' they shall be let alone and not be put to proof?

Qur'án 29:2

Children, repeat after me: *I believe.*
Do the words repulse?
Do you note
a slight constriction of the throat?
A queer racing of the pulse
in sudden fear?
To relieve such symptoms
in their early stages
we find it useful to employ the mind—
how quickly it engages
to assist us here!
Three tiny syllables,
two simple words
of obscure derivation:
is it not absurd
that we feel trepidation?
They're rather less appalling
if when falling from the tongue
you think which syllable is stressed;
this helps divest them of potential harm.
Although you're young
soon you'll learn to say them
without evident alarm.
Three times quickly mumbled,
as with a charm,
they make a pleasant sound,
soothingly jumbled.
Or, more succinctly put,
one may make of them
a kind of verbal rabbit's foot.

One may say the words
attaching mental reservations—
footnote, as it were, one's
private hesitations—
but these, discretion might suggest,
should not be publicly expressed.
It is preferred, of course,
that one pronounce them with
unqualified conviction and with force—
heaven's such a good address
one would not wish to court eviction.
But my meaning, class,
if only you will glean it,
is that one may use the frightening phrase
and, well, not really mean it.
Above all, one should not inflate one's fears
by imagining that as one speaks
the angels are all ears.
One should practice in full privacy.
I've tried saying *I believe*
when quite alone
but felt a choking hand upon my throat—
my own?

THE FORGIVING KIND

*An exercise in litotes, adapted from the reply of an elderly Irish-born pilgrim
to my question: Are you enjoying your pilgrimage?*

Sure that's a lovely little
Universal House of Justice
you have there, Mr White,
they're all such sweet young men.
I suppose that now and then

they find themselves enough to do
to keep them out of mischief. Mind you,
it's not for the likes of me
to tell them what to do
or how to plan
but at eighty-six I've seen a thing or two.
It was the grandest treat to meet them.
Each a fine figure of a man,
I told myself, and all so sweet.
Are you *sure* they get enough to eat?

The Shrines fair blinded me with beauty
and I thought the nice wee
gardens lovely too.
'Well, now,' I told myself, 'it's a
privilege and a duty
to tread these blessed walks
that saw the holy footsteps of your Lord.'
My how a body talks! But I wept, God bless us,
the tears just poured!

At eighty-six, young man, you see
there isn't much time left to me—
and me not hearing of the Holy Faith
till recently
I must catch up for that lost time
I spent in searching.
Not that the fault is mine
entirely, for no one told me
of Bahá'u'lláh till four years ago.
To think that all those years
I searched half blind for want of light
and praying sometimes far into the night

and shedding tears! T'was desperate altogether.
I suppose that God must know
that and forgive me.
The worry of it weighs heavy on my mind.
Ah well, He's the forgiving kind
I tell myself, He'll surely know
I'm not to blame
that all those years
I called aloud to Him in prayer
and did not know His name.
He'd not be one to hold a grudge
but I ask forgiveness all the same . . .

THE INVASION OF ISRAEL BY ESKIMOS

. . . in travelling, a man must carry knowledge with him if he would bring home knowledge.

Samuel Johnson

I

Drifting like the Arctic floe
on which it's said the aged Eskimo
set out to die
the cruise ship comes to harbour,
festive in the face of death.
The geriatric cargo spills ashore,
overfed and overdressed,
in crisp perma-press and spruce drip-dry.
The crowd sheepishly squints,
short of breath,
nauseous with boredom.

The ladies' hair—
gaily tinted Baked-Alaska— glints
beneath their floppy hats
which wilt like sad flowers.
The Hollywood starlet glasses,
defence against more than the sun,
proclaim them tourists
bent on understanding us in several hours.
The women are agile despite their heavy hips.
A crimson crayon was raked
across their ever-moving lips.
The husbands, their pack-asses,
wobbling on spindly legs
in the unaccustomed collegiate clothes
of retirement, sling cameras round their necks,
worry about the safekeeping of their traveller's cheques
and how to pack the trinkets each wife selects.
The men mill like surly bruins
or sleepy children,
tired of lectures, ruins
and Mediterranean extortion.

II

Soon all are whisked with little fuss
to Jerusalem or the Galilee by bus
presumably to see what makes us us.
Nothing holds their interest or can compare
with what they know at home
in Saskatchewan or Arkansas or Delaware.
They complain about the prices
and do not like the terrain or the air.
But time must be put in and it suffices
that they can dispose of this
as just another place they wouldn't care to live.
  Y'know, I really think I'd miss the ice and snow . . .

Give them their due:
what they are offered is not true,
a Disneyland of antiquities and religious sites
soon encompassed *(click!)* in their camera-sights.
    Take one of Mavis on the camel, quick!
They are herded to the bus. One sun-burned
straggler consoles herself: *Think what I've learned!*
The guide who picks his nose is unconcerned.

III

Relieved that it is over
they clamber noisily aboard the ship
to change for dinner.
    I just adored that little church, says Vera,
    but I forget its name.
Harry pours a drink and snorts, *All churches look the same.*
At dinner one remarks that the meals aboard the ship
are the nicest part of any foreign trip.
    We were told it was quite safe to drink the water,
says Baldwin's wife, feeling slightly queasy.
It was always easy to tie her stomach into knots.
The hand reaching for the butter knife
reveals vivid liver spots.
She gives a nervous little pull
at the beads she bought mere hours ago in Istanbul.
    Interesting place! her husband tells his neighbour,
letting a slight silence drop. *But not my sort of place.*
    Quite! is the reply.
The forced cheerfulness masks a sigh. *Well, that's Israel!*
Greece next stop!
One risks a joke and earns his wife's quick frown:
    Y'know, I never thought I'd visit Jesus' home town!
Goldblatt wonders if it would amuse
the stuffy Epsteins if he praised the Arabs, cursed the Jews.

The irony is lost on Miss Kate Connor
who blandly states all people deserve honour.
   I think they over-rate the Mediterranean,
one veteran feels obliged to state. *I prefer*
the Caribbean or the trip around the Cape.
She strokes her unnecessary fur.
The novices are stunned to silence. One brightly chirps,
saving face: *Did you see that place on Mount Carmel—*
   with the golden dome? I meant to ask the tour guide
   if it's someone's home.
Another nods politely and comments how the time has flown.
   We'll see the moon tonight, the weather's clear.
   You like my ring? It's just a souvenir . . .

IV

We are dismissed. They idly chatter on.
When morning comes we find the ship has gone.

SPEAK NO ENGLISH, ME

Speak no English, me he'd said
and I no tongue he owned.
Now, free of the querulous misgivings
to which my pantomimed instructions
had led us the Arab workman and I
sit companionably, on the fringes of friendship,
over a celebratory cup of coffee,
the job well done
despite the wall of incomprehension
across which we had gesticulated helplessly.

All afternoon he'd muttered to himself
rummaging in an abandoned toolbox
for the rusted remnants of English words
he'd learned in school,
sorting and discarding.
Now he presents the sentence he's constructed
from those salvaged odds and ends.

Expansively he gestures
toward my hanging basket-chair:
   Is for sit-down or just for beautiful?

Bravo! I exclaim,
acknowleding his gift,
reflecting that international diplomacy
should be conducted in this way,
without interpreters,
in the truncated dialect of urgency and goodwill,
in the inadequate piercing shorthand of poems.

LANGUAGE

As you move toward me
through the churning crowd
you shed scraps of superstitions,
dark mistrusts,
even as mine fall away
like tattered rags
in the warm brisk zephyr
of your approach.

In one step, two, or ten
I reach you
and we re-enter our own world
which parliaments but guess at.
There is no Jew, no Gentile,
where we meet.

Our smiles give way to wonder
as recollection claims us:
we have no common tongue.
Nakedly languageless,
we cannot take shelter in lies.
Our irrelevant declarations and apologies
lie at our feet in the useless dust.

Your smile returns
lighting your eyes
with lucid hieroglyphics.
Shalom! you say,
grasping my hand.
I watch lexicons move across your lips.

My echoing *Shalom!* strides
across the butchering centuries,
leaps over the ruins of bewildered kingdoms
collapsed on their own fears.

Peace—our only mutual word.
We weigh its taste,
good as the ripened grape,
and embrace in a sanctity of silence
on the seething street.

Ah, friend of my heart,
civilizations have been built of less.
Look! A new world rises in your bright glance;
I see its shining mansions, its holy towers.
In your sigh I hear its music and see,
cradled in your slender hands,
its earliest flowers,
its laws,
its ingathering Book.

LINES FOR A NEW BELIEVER

Et je me demandais: Est-ce assez d'admirer?

Alfred de Musset
Une Soirée perdu

It is not enough to marvel: the sea asks more.
It does not casually strew enticing shells
or call the bronzed athletic family lightly.
There is calculation in its murmur,
frothed treachery laps its shore.

The lonely are lured there
and the timorous lovers
and the lean mad. Oh, who does not adore
the sea! We write our pretty postcards innocently.
Only the pure and grave-eyed children
know its benevolent guile, clutch their sandpails tightly
and do not smile.

Like the solemn children, the dead—
who did not heed the hoarse and reeling gulls—
know that in our darkest incoherence
the ocean spoke, know what it said.
The young ones mark how little we believe,
measure our postured holiday bravura,
our robust joke, but are too young to grieve
for what we have vacated, so keep entitled silence.
It is for us they build the tedious sandcastles,
select a pebble as we leave.
Oh, drop the stone! we snap in sudden violence,
and piously retrieve our litter
(as though the sea by platitude might be placated).
The auspicious pebble dulls.

It is not enough to marvel: the sea asks more.
Let the dreaming, lovely drowned
who loll and bob in bubbled wonder
tell us why, returning,
weeping without sound,
we stand, wistful and incredulous,
along the shore.

THE ARTEFACT

*We must resist the temptation to intellectually distance ourselves from the
living reality of the Cause of God, enclosing it in a glass coffin of our pride's
devising, which we circumambulate admiring our own handiwork.*

William Collins

Unfaithful even to the memory of the appointed hour,
when we found her quietly reposing
on the Isle of Faithfulness, supposing
her a shipwreck victim washed ashore
we carried the frail form to the city,
coffined it in glass— a pity
that such beauty not be seen— and set it
in a place of honour in the central square,
our handiwork and wisdom to adore.

Hers was all loveliness. We came to stare
or lean above her, weeping
that we could not kiss those ever-sleeping lips.
Women tore their hair to see their image
so perfected there and men sobbed
to be incisively reminded that life is robbed
of all our works by undiscriminating death.

Many pressed their mouths upon the cool pane
that could not chafe their lips to desire
or delirious utterance and did not see
beneath the glacial shield the girl's mild bosom
swell with breath, or tears well in her eyes.
None asked what exquisite power she might wield
nor pressed to free her. The thought was raised once
by a dream-fed child but was dismissed as fantasy
by the solemn elders. Such intolerable beauty if alive
could disregulate the city's ordered ways.

Long she lay there and we grew accustomed
to the crystal concentrate of beauty
as the eye to any artefact, placed, marvelled at, forgotten;
but even then some stopped to amaze,
grateful that grace be so contained
as to pose no threat. Opined the local sage,
this age does not deserve her yet.
Well, true enough. Our days have since grown troublesome,
the city swept by plague,
half the population dead or leaving
to take refuge in the hills. Is it absurd
that the heart chills wondering if we erred?
A mournful handful, we have heard,
still circles the englassed prisoner
half-remembering, half-believing.

THE FAIR, FAIR SWANS
Children's Dance Recital, Beit Rothschild, Haifa

Among the pliant forms
there is always one we notice
no less beautiful for its duckling's art
of moving ardently against the beat
in an earnest rapture,
flapping like a distressed kite
that ruptures the precise symmetry
of the monotonously exquisite
gliding nymphs.

At curtain call she stands
flushed in moist surprise
ungainly even in triumph
borrowing her Saturday's-child due
from the parental approbation.
The cascade wraps her in love, in tulle,
brushes her ears as with kisses;
she grows giddy from approval
there among the fair, fair swans.
Is she not now indestructible?

I carefully aim my applause
tossing it like a nosegay
toward her panting figure.
Already her vulnerable eyes glaze and narrow
in sad knowledge that the stage will empty
and the dark wing swallow her.

Let us with beating palms
protract her moment:
has she not redeemed our humble certainty
that wakened from our omnipotent dream
to strain awkwardly oblivious
to the illusive music
we too may dance
while light holds back
the chill dissevering shadow?

RESCUE

Like a bizarre and outsize bird
you teeter on your wind-whipped perch
atop the fifth-storey ledge
at eye level beyond my window,
a mad, bivious boy
declaiming to a world
so glutted with emergencies
it has no time for yours.
Only the wind hears your urgent words.

A performer in your self-created Big Top
you lean outward in studied carelessness
teasing the crowd milling below gaping reproachfully
under the searchlights.

If you see death as your oscillating partner
syntonic in pink tights
spinning toward you through the darkness
with her inviting ambiguous hoop
it is yet the mechanical sirens
of the police and fire cars
that cause you to freeze
in an ambivalence we recognize as our own.

You might spill like a morbid bead
but are threaded by the cord of our attention.
Muted waves of murmured concern float upwards;
the cajoling spokesman of authority
croons through his megaphone.
Cradling your head, you listen
as to a lullaby. Promises rise to stroke you.

Undeservingly, we win you back.
Taut with decision your slim body
turns toward our uncertain love.
Your pale hand waves once in stiff dignity
before you leap toward our tenuous regard
through the net of our applause— to safety?

Restored to anonymity we may ignore you.
The crowd disperses in swift embarrassment
not asking what it was you wished to tell us
that we would not hear.

PART FOUR:

SUFFICIENT EVASION

I trust that I have been sufficiently evasive to make my point clear.
Stanley E. Fish
Self-Consuming Artefacts

Man must learn to bear a certain portion of uncertainty.
Sigmund Freud

A WHITE BIRD

A white bird calls across the water
In the faint light where I wait alone.
The low cool notes float whitely muted,
Naked as bone.

I cup the echo in a seashell,
Press its lips against my cautious ear.
Soft in the breathy kissing murmur
One name I hear.

A rush of wings above the water
In the darkness where I stand alone.
At my feet a small white feather falls
And a smooth white stone.

A distant whir of wings receding,
A shadow swiftly swoops across the moon.
I place the round pale pebble on my tongue—
It tastes of *soon*.

WHY DO YOU COME NOW, GLISTENING?

Why do you come now, glistening
   like the dissilient persimmon—
you who left me so long a beggar—
   come now, when I am worn coin-thin
by palming of the pedlars of the scrunt mad-apple
   in the seething, carnal market?

Why do you come now, beckoning,
   and garlanded, and speaking words of love—
you who stood serenely cowled in shadow
   on the periphery of vision,
disdainful as death,
   estranged by moonlight
as I circumambulated your remoteness, weeping?
   I heard the taunting whisper of your silks,
knew the piercing musk of your white violets.
   Did you not hear me call your name, fainting with desire?
Too late, too late you come to madefy the desert,
   tenderly strewing petals.
My flowers long ago gave way to thorns.
   Can you not see my rags and tatters?

Why do you come now, smiling,
   with urgent outstretched arms
and incautious fingers feeding in my hair?
   Your soft lips brush my stricken throat—
not they nor your low lush moans revive my voice
   grown husk and dry with betrayal and dissimulation.
Well I know you would lead me to the scented circinate pavilion
   high above the green sea's muted murmur;
I know the ambient garden dishevelled by luxuriance
   where you would sing to me—
I who live in sand and couch on stone.
   What would you have me do, who can no longer dance or sing?

Why do you come now, profoundly,
   distraught with marvels,
brimming with promises and bright words—
   come with the innocence of morning
with your compelling shoulders,
   your unloosed negligent robe—
now; now that I have forgotten you,
   forgotten your forgiving eyes
and the long years' famine?

Would you have me sob against your breast:
Ah! Do not abandon me, beloved, my dearly-desired,
   my long-awaited one!
   Would you charge me with neglect?

Why do you come now, pleading,
   when I have disposed of recollection,
relinquished your light cascading laughter,
   your vulnerable pale thighs—
now, when I will not have you stay—
   now when I move ardently toward the black and birdless
   thicket where you cannot follow?
   Go . . .

A TOAST TO THE HERO

The in-flight thriller tells likable lies.
Expansive with airborne wellbeing
we loosen our belts and suspend disbelief
eagerly gullible to the technicolour manipulation
content with the violence,
the predictable victory,
the lovers' final torrid clinch.
We do not question how the hero arrives
bandbox fresh from the transoceanic flight
and two frames from the runway
hurtles off in the sleek sportscar
to rendezvous at the luxurious flat
of the compliant mysterious blonde
with the unplaceable accent
and the inviting double bed;
acquiesce to the convoluted intrigue,
the syncopated chase,
the shrugged-off triumph
when the villains fall like dandruff.

Oh so to edit our lives
as to always emerge in celluloid safety
incapable of less than the toothpaste-ad-smile finish!
How gallantly the unrecriminatory girl
will see the hero go—*eet vas fun, chéri*—
too sensible to speak about commitment.

The screen is scrubbed of the colossal lie.
The stewardess in an aura of feigned promiscuity
adjusts our pillows, offers us a drink.
Let us gratefully toast the impeccable hero.
Without the tedium of his choiceless invulnerability
would we be content to descend
stopped-eared at O'Hare or Heathrow,
giddy with jetlag, stomach in revolt,
longing to launder the denture,
glad of the predictable wonder
of our ordinary lives,
unscripted and flawed and plausible,
gloating at the ease with which
we smuggle through Customs with the souvenirs
our small dutiable failures,
our undeclared guilts,
the incalculably priceless booty of our human joy?

CONFRONTATION

Athena: Yet these, too [the Furies] have their work . . .

The Eumenides

Despite our chaste abstractions
she boisterously intrudes,
do as we will to keep her afar.

Damp, ridiculous, demanding,
she rumples our silence like bedsheets,
wantonly dismissing every bar,

her exasperating presence
a strident trespass. The tone,
limp hair and untidy gestures jar.

She has brought flowers. Spilling petals
and ash she sprawls possessively,
shoes off, strums the guitar

then leans on the fastidious bookshelf,
slovenly, gap-seamed and garrulous,
her voice coarse, her words bizarre

— all an extravagant tumult.
No! we protest, it *cannot* be like that!
She shrugs and grins: *It is. I am. You are.*

ELEGY

The sun cannot protract its stay,
though it spreads its argument vividly
across the water. It leaves reluctantly the
voluptuous trees whose green contours
it had caressed, and the soft fields
where it tumbled playfully
among anemonies and Queen Anne's lace.
Even the sullen hills, rigidly puritanical,
whose only grace is stone,
darken thoughtfully at this departure
gazing to the waves
where the last tatters of colour fade.
You sieze my hand in urgent announcement.
Darling, you say, *look! The moon!*
and do not speak of danger.

STAR-GAZER

In my brain's stark firmament
There ride no stars but two.
One I dare to guess is God
And one I named for you.

Often I've supposed them wink
And pondered what I'll lose
If in some sharp extremity
A voice commands me choose.

Of what use were eternity
If I household there alone?
What use earth's domesticity
If cost of that be home?

One compelling orb will dim
When sounds the austere voice.
What shuddering unsung death attends
This sole and ruthless choice?

YOUNG MAN, OLD MAN

How shall I love, and I so young,
And you beyond my clasping?
How shall I thrive or give hope tongue
Who know this cruellest fasting?

How shall I live, and I grown old,
And heaven an unscanned sea?
Life, with you far past my hold,
Proved death enough for me.

RECOVERY

The child vanished like a bubble
when his world split
to bury him with crushing rubble.
Calmly, tight-lipped
we dig for him among the ruins
these long years after.
His faint cry leads us. If he now assumes
forgiving laughter,
drinking light,
he will not forget
nor reclaim innocence.
Dust rims his startled brows and lashes, yet
gulping sun his flinty gaze relents
and the rescuer knows dazzling grief
as the boy's sealed lips move
shedding with each word
a moldering leaf.
He speaks of love.

A MAIDEN'S PRAYER

Data to be fed into a computer dating system

I

I long to have a pale green pond
In which cool lillies float,
A tangled maze, a drawbridge,
And to challenge my love, a moat.

Rosebeds to lure the brave lad on,
A thorn hedge of great length,
A dragon with a fiery breath
To test the dear boy's strength.

A tall stout vine to tempt the prince
To scale the turret wall,
A silk-lined sleeping chamber
And a carved bed, narrow, small.

Chaste jasmine at the lattice
To spur the youth's attack,
An Iron Maiden in dank vault
And a dainty prince-sized rack.

II

I yearn to have a cottage,
O let the roof be thatched!
With whitewashed walls and ample door,
Bright red, and never latched.

Blue crockery on a clean pine shelf,
Brass kettle on the boil,
A well-scrubbed floor, the larder full,
A garden where I'll toil.

A bed— O please! One large and wide
As would invite kind dreams,
Where lovers nestled in the dark
Might speak the soul's own themes.

Neat panes with shutters thrown wide
To coax sun's light to stay,
A clear path to the wide-flung door
To speed true love my way.

THE KISS

I

The palace gained, he nimbly found
The chamber where she couched spell-bound
And having read the tale, he knew
All his kiss empowered to do.

His amorous eyes gazed long and deep
At innocence so locked in sleep
As never love's sore cost to pay.
He sighed and left her where she lay.

II

Through castle halls he dully lumbered,
By chance found where the lady slumbered.
He stole a kiss (he thought on whim,
Not having read the Brothers Grimm.)

The maiden slowly raised her eyes,
Exclaiming 'Is this paradise?'
Then drew her first unstupored breath
And roused to love and pain and death.

WAITING

I does not matter that you look
Your most engaging; that the book
You idly leaf is well approved
To tell your wit. He is not moved.

The dust beneath your lounge chair curls
Unnoticed as the graceful swirls
Of your sleeve's tumult as you reach
To stroke your hair or choose a peach

Or tint again with kiss-proof red
Your willing lips or stroke the bed
So guilelessly arranged, as though
Not accomplice to your hope. Throw

Back your head before the glass
Rehearsing faces. Time will pass
But note how waiting wears away
A beauty never meant to stay.

Perhaps another dress? But no,
Soft blue is right, persuading so
Discreetly in the cup of breast
That virtue clings there, love finds rest.

From crystal vase the petals spill;
Sweep them swiftly, if you will,
Remarking how the faultless rose
Too soon exhaustedly explodes

Silently, as though the weight
Of its perfection detonates.
How might the telephone not ring
When you glide by? Such grace could bring

Marvelling strangers to your door
Or dazzled lovers to implore
The hand and heart you'd quickly give,
Both blameless as the life you live;

Impeccable, as every room
That you possess. Against hushed gloom
Of stealthy dusk light cheerful tapers,
Warm the wine, while Chopin capers

In flourished étude on your set,
Gay counterpoint to your regret
As night slinks blackly toward your pane
To watch you dine alone again.

No word or gesture, thought or call,
You wait in vain for his footfall.
Toast smiling, madam, this delay—
The guest comes soon; too long his stay.

METAMORPHOSIS AND MARRIAGE

I

Sure I read Dan Jordan's 'Becoming your true self.' But what does he know about frogs?

The Frog

The princess when she heard my plea
Great horror did evince.
Why should a girl believe it
When a frog says he's a prince?

She bravely put her lips to mine
And broke the cursed spell,
Invited me to call on her
And grew to love me well.

I moved into her castle then
And led a jolly life;
It is a lucky frog who has
A princess for his wife.

She soon grew fat and querulous
And now seeks a divorce.
Detesting scandal, I refuse—
I've much to lose, of course.

Why should a charming chap like me
Return to live in ooze?
I've now a taste for soft clean beds,
Home cooking and good booze.

Besides, young maidens comfort me
And these I soon convince
I only dreamed I was a frog
But always was a prince.

The princess sorrows night and day
But my heart she'll not wring.
What more deserves a girl who'd kiss
An ugly, warted thing?

II

Don't kiss the frogs in this pond, girls . . . they turn into husbands!
The Princess

When first the monster raised his cry,
Fantastic as it seems,
I thought my kiss had power to yield
The prince of all my dreams.

I pressed the slithering lips to mine
(I blanch to think of it!)
There stood, transformed, a handsome man
All grace and charm and wit.

I could but love the dashing prince
Born of my generous kiss,
So took him home to change his life
From loneliness to bliss.

I hung new curtains all around.
The castle looked most gay.
I put perfume behind my ears
And wore a *négligé*.

But soon, I learned, does love grow chill
When beauty marries beast
If he feels for benefactress
Not grateful in the least.

Glad I'd be for pity's sake
Again to wield my powers
But he seeks metamorphosis
In a hundred women's bowers.

He still remains a frog, I fear,
And sometimes I delight
To hear his tortured croaking
Echo through the lonely night.

MARK'S MADRIGAL

There are two hells: marriage and celibacy. Take your choice.

Mark Tobey

Breathes there the man so limp with dread
Who never of his wife hath said,
'I love the wench but wish her dead!'
Quia amore langueo.
I am sick with love.

O lissom lass, O languid lad,
In wedlock are love's lessons had.
Were freedom gained, what is allowed
But from a stranger's hand a shroud?

Lives there the woman so unsound
Who never thought, in marriage bound,
'I'll sleep best when he's underground!'
Quia amore langueo.
I am sick with love.

O noble lady, gallant knight,
Find ye in wedlock full delight
For all are granted fleeting terms
And restive are the amorous worms.

Exist there spouses, common–law,
Who never felt the question gnaw,
"What chain hath love that rubs me raw?'
Quia amore langueo.
I am sick with love.

Both winsome maid and handsome squire
Know love's the chief prize we acquire
But count it, wed or celibate,
A hellish torment, soon or late.

'Tis not the mate by whom we're soured
But love itself which proves us coward.
To tame the fear's to tame the fire,
'Tis fear of love of which we tire.

Have done, good folks, with suffering,
Brave choice secures diviner thing.
Love won by courage shall endure
For love, methinks, is love's own cure.
Rejoice, rejoice in love!

THE COUP

For Mimi and Ting

Classification: phylum Chordata,
subphylum Vertebrata, class Mammalia,
order Carnivora, family Felidae.

Content yourselves, whiskered ones, with the tidy definition,
The lisped 'pretty puss', the insulting catnip mouse;
It costs nothing to humour their servile condition.
Remember, ours is an ancient and distinguished house.

Poor furless frightened things! Dear
It cost us when their hate-engendering brain
To exorcise its talent for evil, fashioned its obscene fear
In our shape; with the innocent witch our forbears died in pain.

Worse was our well-warranted veneration.
Such damned-fool requests gods have put to them!—
Make the woman love me! Bless and redeem this generation!—
Thus were we asked to subsidize the laziness of men.

Permit them the neutral entry. Our oral history
Tells what it tells of their terror of their own divinity
And vice. They cower before our mystery
Fawning and fainting in hoped-for affinity.

And are so easily distracted and amused!
We need only look inscrutable or arch the back
And they sink to servitude. Ah, we are not much abused,
My almond-eyed. Bide patiently. One day we will attack.

Their self-willed wars will fell them, their perversion
And their lack of love. It will be a bloodless coup
For us, the unpedigreed or purebred, the Manx, the Persian,
The Siamese, the Abyssinian, the Russian Blue—

The world will be given us through default of evolution
So retract your claws, look charmingly feline;
In our midnight councils (so misunderstood!) we vetoed revolution.
Hush! Frisk winsomely— the servant comes— we dine.

All together, now: *meow*.

SPENDTHRIFT

There is a tradition in Islám that on the Last Day, in response to the divine call Am I not your Lord? *two* yeses *(Arabic: Na'mayn or Na'amayn) will be heard. Cf.* Qur'án *7:172*

One yes I thought to squander
And one to keep in store
And I like child a-penny-rich
The fraught choice did deplore;
But spent I one and spent I well
Nor counted love's cost sore—
Yet note the dole replenished,
Two yeses still my hoard,
And smile to think what is secured
By double assent, Lord.

THE OTHER SHORE

Let us not stroke too swiftly toward
   the green opposite shore
where death rehearses. We have tried these
   pearl-promising waves before
and might guess the danger.

Recall how always we turn back spent
   to the sun-warmed sand
and stand anguished in separate solitudes,
   though hand in hand,
each to each grown stranger.

Not that the brave bird lied. But that
   we, young, too soon said
Land! Land! and, plunging, did not see
   his torn pinion, his bloodied head.
Ease us, wise love, toward this wet danger.

FOR THE CHILDREN, WATCHING

*On reading of the attempt by a man in Germany in August 1979 to end his
life by leaping from a window. He fell upon two children playing in the street
below, killing one and injuring the other. The man, although injured, lived.*

Children, we must watch the sky,
not as the ancients did, fearfully,
lest the gods express electric disapproval
or Vesuvius disgorge a lethal wrath;
not for the annihilating mushroom
or the bomber's metal messages.

The plague will spread invisibly
from the sleek commercial plane's effluvium
despite our wary gaze
and disbelief will not arrest
the bizarre Icarian plunge of the suicide
falling upon us from the scaffold of his despair
as we lean innocently to scoop our marbles.
Shall we cower
as night swarms in
to smother with forgiveness
the precise or random murders
which our elegant indignation cannot stay
while the mollificatory stars
look on unabashed in pregnant constellation?

It were wiser to stand in Magian silence,
reverent before the admonishing blackness,
and read in its long dark reign
the gathering of an astounding dawn.
Let us watch the sky, children,
incautious with hope,
jubilant with wisdom.

HUNGER

Ah love, you were too soon to die.
My need could not detain you;
But quick my smile and dry my eye
Lest my fare of grief arraign you.

Ah life, you were too long to live
For one who'd dine on laughter.
Sparse nourishment the slow years give
Tells timeless feast hereafter.

PRIMER FOR A NEW DAY: *1979 UN INTERNATIONAL YEAR OF THE CHILD*

Please do not force your child to read this or any other book. Reading should always be a very happy experience.

Introduction to a child's first reader

In the primers of our childhood they had names
like Dick and Jane or Pam and Basil, and we hated them,
hated their privileged, relentless jollity and laboured precocity.
Calamity was their pet, Spot, treeing a cat (naughty dog!)
or tapioca pudding for dessert
met with a permitted wry grimace and (such wit!)
a sniggered 'fish-eyes-and-glue!'
We never spoke as they did:
  See the ball. The ball is red. Red, red, red.

We envied them their fancy schools and family car,
their well-placed pallid parents, permissive as Christmas,
secure as banks, who had never learned to traumatize,
so nicely neutered it could be imagined
they acquired their loathsome progeny by mail order
or had them installed with the tasteful furniture
by an impeccable decorator.
Yet to have earned that approbation or one 'Well done!'
we would have become achievers, adopted the endearing smile,
the ingratiatingly game attitude, attended the merry picnic
and never let the home team down.
  Dick can jump. See him jump. Jump, jump, jump.

Their mother pleaded 'Not now, darling, or mommy will be
cross,' and fled from distress
with sick headaches to bed in full daylight.
The women we knew spoke our true names, felt real anger,
worked through their sicknesses, somehow endured.
Their father, vague as a sleepwalker,
daily vanished like a shadow to some unspecified task,
was never out or sorts or lacking manly counsel.
Ours had blistered hands, knew exhaustion,
towered like giants, uttered oaths
raising their voices like gods. Their labour bought our food.
We coveted the bland glamour of those children's parents.
Who would not have traded ours for theirs, or sought their
praise?
   Look, Father, Jane can skip. Skip, skip, skip.

Our mothers being black or red, Irish, or Polish Jews,
might have worked in their kitchens,
fed us their humiliating table scraps,
described the gazebo and the croquet set.
We could have forgiven their immunity to poverty
but not to pain and disappointment,
not their complacent command of existence,
their innocence of headcolds, hand-me-downs
and the more shameful staining orifices,
not their unquestioning assumption of entitlement to life,
that perfect and casual power.
   Dick and Jane have fun at school. School is fun, fun, fun.

While they spent summers by cool northern lakes
at peachy-keen camps with Indian names
we vacationed in our tree-huts— but not all of us had trees.
Our cooling came from lawn hoses or hydrants
   or the ice-man's cart.
O dimpled darlings, had a cynic told us
there were cockroaches in your pantry
we would have assumed your mother ordered them from
   Tiffany (in cloisonné, with jewelled eyes)
or inherited them from a doting aunt
with the Georgian heirloom tea service.
   How can we forgive your
having almost persuaded us that life was or should be
   one long indulgence?
   Dick likes cake. Jane likes cake, too. Cake, cake, cake.

Well, children, if you are out there in the shrinking world
you will probably have noticed the writing on the wall.
Not everyone is content to think the times outgrew you
and those who invented you
and we who envied the lie that was your life;
not all accept that you got older, married, divorced,
harbour cancer or succumbed to liquor or despair.
An ardent few still feel they have a score to settle,
some with guns and violence. You, too, have heard
the night sirens, the startled cries of terror that rend
the soft fabric of summer evenings
in the most unalarming and discreet suburbs.
   Children, do you sleep with fear? Fear, fear, fear.

Ah Jane, Ah Dick! The world we held as lightly
as you your imperishably gay red ball
spins drunkenly, inflames, seethes with menace.
Our time skids away on its own falsehoods and now
the page grows blear, the candle gutters,
suicide to its own tears.

To what book does sorrow point us
as would dignify our suffering and yet not force our gaze?
If heaven holds calligraphy to tell this day
may we not see the dawn-spawned words *through pain, rebirth*
and being human hope as humans must?
Released from slogans and their blood-stained past
what simple bracing words
contain the heart's true image:
Hope! Faith! Wonder! Love! Renewal!

Children, shall we not be happy as we learn to read the age?

WHOM LOVE BLINDS

for Catherine M'boya

Black was she
and white was he,
love bathed their hours with colour.

Fate's bleaching whim
wrenched her from him
and oh! their lives were duller.

Grief's swart dye
stained his mind's eye,
his pitch world lacked all lightness.

Tear-blinded, she
could only see
his absence as a whiteness.

LEDA'S SONG

Did she put on his knowledge with his power
Before the indifferent beak could let her drop?

W. B. Yeats
Leda and the Swan

Well knew I, women, my winged love was divine
When feigning faint I sank at feathered thrust
In glad cognition that I, a thing of dust,
Might yielding win his wisdom or make mine
Some part of his power; at least to know
That I attract a god were truth enough
For courage. Freely I clung kissing that strange ruff
Grazing my breast until he let me go
Whirling away in brilliant dazzlement.
I, left to mortal loneliness and loss, crept
Weeping to my huband's bed and except
I betrayed the god with him had no content.
A bleak forked knowledge I assumed that day—
Faithless to god, impatient now of clay.

LINES ON AN UNLAMENTED DEATH

The boy was unadept at living, so he died—
it was that simple— quite unlamented.
He was gauche, asocial, perhaps demented.
Dancing in lifts and trams! Can it be denied
his ways were strange? Once he leapt upon
a small low table and burst into song;
shocked the guests and caused the host vexation.
Such lack of discipline, such meagre pride!
He should have known the act and impulse wrong.
Excess of joy, he gave as explanation.
He favoured the extreme, the rash, the wild.
We never trusted him for he was sly;
we counselled, but he would not meet our eye—
was prankful, teasing— well, very like a child.

It's known that he liked flowers, wrote poems, too,
and painted— we dare not guess what more!—
he'd prate of love and dreams and weep at beauty.
We hoped he'd see that this would never do—
how many times we turned him from our door!
(We bore him no ill will, but saw our duty.)
He met a bloodless, silent end, we'd guess;
murdered, it's thought, though some claim suicide.
And not a word about it in the press—
well, having none, that would not slight his pride.
He's dead, let's leave it there—we're spared disgrace.
I cannot mourn—I wear his slaughtered face.

NUNCIO

*The poems of Roger White are marred by an apocalyptic intuition and an
excess of personal conviction incompatible with the contemporary literary
taste. It would be extremely difficult to place his poems in a literary journal.*
(letter from the editor of a Canadian poetry journal)

All a poet can do today is warn.

Wilfred Owen.

With feather not with hammer
I would wish to lightly brush
the sleep-fast windows of a dozing world
where our unwitting brother lies innocently curled
while the flames leap lush
and the rank winds yammer.

A croon might fix the sleeper's dream
to char swiftly with his ashes
and lift forlornly to drift in sodden dawn
void-bound, traceless, forever gone.
Tongues lick the door, lap the sashes.
Wingless, I clamber; songless, scream.

FIGURES IN A GARDEN

The essence of true safety is to observe silence, to look at the end of things and to renounce the world.

Bahá'u'lláh
Words of Wisdom

The speakers are the Persian poet Ṭáhirih (1817/18–1852) and the American poet Emily Dickinson (1830–1886)

. . . just as the rays of the natural sun have an influence which penetrates into the darkest and shadiest corners of the world, giving warmth and life even to creatures that have never seen the sun itself, so also, the outpouring of the Holy Spirit through the Manifestation of God influences the lives of all, and inspires receptive minds even in places and among peoples where the name of the Prophet is quite unknown.

J. E. Esslemont
Bahá'u'lláh and the New Era

I

Ṭihrán, Persia, 1852

> The very name is fragrant,
> slides silkily across the tongue
> and I weep in knowledge of it
> as I once wept in longing to know it.
> It has the good of honey on the mouth,
> this name— a flame in the mind,
> and its echo in the burning heart
> a cool sweet water. Drink of my heart,
> I would tell them. Drink and know his name!
> Be nourished of the knowledge of the Lord!
> It becomes an easy thing to die
> with this name on the lips,
> this ultimate feast. I who loved sweets
> now given this, the nectar of figs!
> I speak while there is yet time.

Children, children, forgive me,
but I have known the poem made manifest,
shall I deny the author?
And if your father cast me away,
shall I deny the verse?
And if I be driven from the land,
could I ignore the book?
Do not imagine I overlook the danger
of the name, this greatest branding.
It is a jeopardous career the lover chooses
and the master's ownership forever marks the slave.

From the uncurtained niche I would tell this name
or from the minaret. Scholars, servants, sisters—
all would I tell, till my tongue be silenced
and my companions be the stones.
They, too, I would have know, and the cypress,
and the sea. Into a million million bottles
would I seal the name and send them in
the waves' white hands to all the corners
of the world. And deserts cross and mountains climb
to breathe it to the deaf sand and the proud eagle.
Observe how this intoxicant assassinates
all dusty loyalties.

Come with me, husband! Give me the strength
of your firm arm. Join me, children, light my path
with flowers and your laughter.
Are you content to be stones?
Let us streak across the firmament
like maddened comets!

They do not hear. Doors close.
Then my tears will be my progeny
and I shall string abuse into a necklace
to adorn my throat. If I wrench off my veil
it will be to tear the indifferent eyelid
of a sleeping world and if I die
my pale face will imprint itself on the moon
and float above the world announcing his name
to those who would read.

Mark me, women, my compass is set for madness.
The pole of *Am I not Thy Lord?* is my magnet
and I its *Verily, Thou art!* None shall stay this course.
The passage will be stormy, women,
watch it well and pray.
The sea before us is of blood
and its dolphins the severed heads of lovers.
I could lend you courage if you lean on me.

Listen! The sea speaks!
Put down your needles and listen, sisters,
the sea speaks my name.
Soon you shall see where its tumult
will carry my craft and marvel that
it sweeps me to a garden where
my song will end.
I shall go from home no more
but shall wear a white gown
and choose silence.

Amherst, Mass., 1853

I shall not go from home
but shall wear a white gown
and choose silence
and my world will be my garden.
I shall fit myself to the small contours
of my life as a meek accommodating moss
crochets itself about a stone
and in the silence there shall speak
that intimation that nudges the mind in dreams
which my stirring lashes banish
as they lift reluctantly to light.

If the village declares me mad
I shall offer no defence.
Twigs of gossip will catch at my skirt
as I move toward the alyssum at dusk
to breathe its scent dim as memory
but unconcerned I shall stoop
to press my face in its cool circle
mysterious as a footprint
from which I conjure the sped quarry.
Taunts will gather in my hem
unnoticed as lint and if mocking laughter
insinuates itself through the evening air
my slim hand will brush it away absently
as it would the frail architecture
of the tenant of lilacs which
intimidates stickily my face.
It is not the spider I seek here
though we are sisters in industry.

Eternity sweeps around me like a sea
lapping me with sounds
that drown the braggart heartbeat
and the fatuous pulse
leaving me weak and grateful.
One word I ask, one name— speak!
I would make my home in the
green palace of the sea's voice
but she gives back only murmurous sighs
drenching me with her sad reluctances
dearer than the sun's noon-day avowals
which the strident crow has by rote.
One word would be inundation
if it came from the sea!

My heart grows as still
as the lilac's dark leaves.
What name does my love wear?
They rustle in opaque reverence
but do not tell
and now the sky's silver aborigine
slips from the ribcage of the trees
to ride quietly in the black lake overhead
tantalizing me with her calm authority
and faint hieroglyphics carved by pain,
a halo to my madness.
Tell, mother, tell!
But love or terror has silenced the moon
and her eyes are incontinent as mine.
Where is he? What have they done to my Lord?
A cloud modestly veils her wan face
and in shame I draw my questions
about me like a cloak and move toward the house
where the bright rooms chirrup with trivia,
simmer with responsibilities.

Tomorrow when the tawny moths gather
to embroider the twilight
I shall steal again to the garden
to beg the moon to yield up her immortal secret,
to implore the sea to spell the perfumed name
that its accents may inhabit my silence
and my soul dissolve as its syllables find admittance.

POLLUX TO CASTOR

Now having come this far shall we go on?
You, dear, not dead and I but half alive
And weary, who think it easier to pawn
Divinity for respite than to strive
Against you in a dual so finely drawn
With yours a subtler skill, mine stronger steel.
How shall I gather heart for further bout;
What paean sing to kindle pulse and nerve—
(Who with but sloe-eyed glance you quickly rout
And with one kiss enslave)? Would my death serve?
Oh one must die, beloved, have no doubt
This stern and fixed decree grants no appeal.
God's very sky the gift your death will win—
Prepare to die, my love, my foe, my twin.

NEWS FROM THE FRONT

Citizens, the brave bird did not lie
But we shall stone him,
For he, announcing life, deserves to die.
Set to it with a robust will;
We know him true
but will not own him. Let
None ask is it ourselves we kill.
Not even the toothless fools
In the Temple praying
Busy with beads and book
Remark this slaying.

What need we care
If the sky grows dark at noon,
Our sons brood idly
And our women weep
In the heavy stinging air?
It is not too soon
To aim the silencing blow.
Will life not keep?

Let the winging raven come
And blight our fields
Where the sheaves pale
And no cricket's heard
To welcome his sooty reign.
What if our wells fail
And no orchard yields;
Who will complain, my countrymen,
That we had a use for life
Or singing bird?

PART FIVE:

THUMBNAIL SKETCHES

See ye no strangers; rather see all men as friends, for love and unity come hard when ye fix your gaze on otherness.

'Abdu'l-Bahá

Our task is to learn how to meet the inner spirit of the people, and not just revolve around and around their outer personality.

Horace Holley

The individuality of each sister is to be respected. There is more than one mould of holiness. Each life is precious.

St Catherine of Bologna
1413–1463

NOTES MADE IN A DARKROOM

I see them through the eye of fear
And envy them their beauty;
Yet when in love's lens they appear
They're cherished as mere duty.

Viewed through yet another glass
The focus grows unclouded;
Each wears my face and walks my path,
The destination shrouded.

Bathed in balance are light and shade,
Attraction and repulsion,
Distortion-free the image made,
Eternal the emulsion.

LINES FOR A BIGOT

It's easy to spot one of *those*,
They've a roman, hooked or button nose.
Always they're rather thin or fat—
Or average, if it comes to that.
Their eyes will quickly give the clue:
Hazel, green, grey, brown or blue.
They're dusky and swart or pale and wan
With hair that's light or dark or gone
And always kinky, curled or straight,
Their clothes high-styled or out-of-date.
If they're not florid and verbose
They're mildly sociable or morose.
Of all their traits I most deplore
Their being this way, that way, or . . .

BILLIE'S BLUES

The blues ain't nothing but a pain in the heart . . .

Billie Holiday

With microphone the dark queen stands.
We note the stillness of her hands,
The beaten stance, the vacant eye—
O sing us, Billie, as we die.

The voice caressed by saxaphone
A frightened child's who's lost its home;
The stumbling songs too well explain
The colour, texture, shape of pain.

She halts as though the sobbing air
Might not withstand the knife she'll bare.
Describe the anguish love can give;
Lament us, Billie, as we live.

PICNIC AT THE HILTON

Take it from me, Mavis,
you meet a lot of loonies
in a hotel job.
They swagger in, y'know,
dressed to the nines
and acting like butter wouldn't melt.
But you can't judge by appearances.
It isn't enough that you're short staffed
and dying from the ankles down,
you have to put up with
the goings-on behind locked doors.
The world's full of oddballs
and sooner or later
they check in here.

The old doll in 703, like.
The bellhop tipped me off—
said her suitcase *rattled*.
And her looking like someone's
sweet old aunt from Biloxie,
the kind who'd keep a pet canary
and never forget your birthday.
But a rattling suitcase!
I mean, it could make a girl nervous.

So I go in to check the linen, see,
the end of my shift and my feet killing me,
and the old girl's having a party,
guests all over the room
enjoying a regular picnic.
She was toting a hotplate and dishes in her bag!
Made me kind of chuckle.
Not a penny-pincher, mind—
the hospitality of the thing, see?
I'm standing there thinking it takes all kinds,
and the old bird smiles.
Welcome, dearie, she says, *come in and meet my friends.*
You look tired, would you like a cup of tea?
It got me, y'know. I nearly cried—
see, I haven't been on a picnic
since I was a kid.

Take it from me, Mavis,
you get your share of loonies
but you meet some swell people in a hotel job.

BARRED ENTRY

Not every one that saith unto me, Lord, Lord, shall enter into the kingdom of heaven . . .

Matt. 7:21

She is owned by voices not her own,
their origin forgotten;
speaks with the bleak, didactic hostility
of a mission tract
assuming in arrogant resignation
the world unsalvageable,
its irremediable sinfulness
requisite support to her self-esteem.

Substanceless, without a sovereign centre,
she pantomimes humility,
seethes with unctuous pieties,
vents torrents of amorphous platitudes
in flabby parody of an elation she has never known;
pores over scripture in wheezing anxiety
but the seminal words do not rise from the page
to enter her gangrenous soul
barricaded from faith by her conviction of achievement.
Her flagellant prayers, offered to an invisible jury
which tries her on unstated charges,
describe aspirations she feels at second hand.

She traffics in ingratitude,
spends herself on the unrescuable and doggedly doomed
who do not by acquiescence
threaten her precarious superiority.
In their eventual desertion
she finds pleasurable martyrdom,
blots her steamy, vaporous eyes
and bemoans human intractability
but does not recognize her gratification.
Never has she afforded the luxury of laughter,
a deserved *no,* one heartfelt *go to hell;*
buys uneasy peace with accusatory charities
compulsively dispensed to chosen ingrates.
In the forcing-house of her asphyxiating inverse virtue
all life must wither and love malignantly mutate.

Alone with her terror
she is stalked by strangulating shadows
that menace from the corners of her room.
God is love! she protests aloud with sudden vehemence.
The compassionate silence that might hold healing
splits before the force of her rage from which,
their grace unsought, the powerless angels flee weeping.
In the engulfing darkness
her possessing prideful voices
cackle malevolent approval.

OLD MEN ON SUMMER EVENINGS

In the shadows, two by two,
Strolling lovers claim youth's due,
The silk sheet of the evening air
Drawn just for them, so thinks each pair.

Each couple's watched by grave old men
Whose time has passed and come again
(Night's sheet for them portent of shroud)
Who ask is flesh but *this* allowed—

A fevered moment in the shade,
A yielding woman's answer made,
The soul exhaled in one swift kiss?
The perjurious blood cries *Only this!*

Kind stars to ease such limp regret
Potently signal: *And yet . . . and yet . . .*

MINOR ARTIST

for Dotan Uziel

The six-year old in interview,
Pressed to account for all he drew
Which inspired the adult critics' awe,
Shrugged patiently: 'I *like* to draw.'

'When you grow up what will you be,
An artist?' (asked patronizingly—
How tolerant children are of us!)
'I'm an artist *now*. I'll drive a bus.'

THE LAST INNOCENT

*. . . while I see that there is nothing wrong in what one does, I see that there
is something wrong with what one becomes. It is well to have learned that.*
Oscar Wilde

After the long hours of nursing watered drinks
among the pretty capering boys
the last bar disgorges him
on the tawdry street where the butch day
has unclenched its fist and night sprawls,
dark and voluptuous,
to feed his soft fantasy.

Don't do anything I wouldn't do!
he calls to the giggling youth
who pair in unlikely liaisons
and will do everything
that might persuade them they are loved.
Don't trip on your train, Duchess!
shrieks one, so young and lovely
as never to have imagined limitation.

Too, too camp! The litany of insult
now a reflex. And waddles away
in the loneliness of sixty,
his plump hips swaying in habitual invitation,
mincing in imagined stiletto heels
toward a fabulous camera
his mind providing the black reels
that record some major epic.
*Take six, Miss Hepburn. Elizabeth has
sent you to the tower. You turn,
a tragic, regal figure . . .*

Dimmed shopfronts give back his image
assuaged to his liking,
neon and streetlights play in the blond rinse
of his thin teased hair.
Now all scenarios are possible.

He is legendary.
Slender, elegant and enigmatic,
in an apocalypse of flashbulbs
he auditions a voice, *I want to be alone,*
shudders at the lie,
his aloneness so irrevocably achieved.

A stoplight halts his courtly progress,
its red authority conjuring a defiant vamp.
Hand on hip he frisks the eyes
of an indifferent cop, *Come up and see me sometime,*
finds pleasure in the tender/tough persona.
Imagination furnishes an ermine wrap,
a sequin gown. Limousines pant in readiness
to whisk him to Grauman's, a penthouse assignation,
a speakeasy of the underworld.
The world of fashion trembles at his choices,
tycoons and poets fear his every frown
and bellhops effect his ruin in sodden dreams.

But none can loathe him as he loathes himself.
He winks at the whistled homage
of hulking streetboys
jeering from the safety of gangs
keyed to distraction by blue movies and
adolescent doubt. But he is not their prey.
Sniffs disdainfully at the casual costly cowboys
who lurk in doorways to advertise
their theatrical maleness
packaged in straining denim.
Get you, dearie!

Nothing so obvious tempts him from
his fastidious course.

He dreams of a greater humiliation—
forced at gunpoint by an escaped convict—
the gown torn, one breast helplessly
exposed to the rough hand,
the gasped protest and swooning surrender;
or seduction of the ultimate innocent,
freckled and fresh from the fields,
virgin to women and hot for centrefolds.
So you don't have a girlfriend?
But sighs. There are no more innocents.
And so returns to innocence himself
who knows no self to be.
Alone in the All-Nite Diner,
stark as a confessional,
the brutal mirror, unable to support illusion,
bludgeons him with truth.
He fights back tears,
tells the blowzy sympathetic waitress—
a geriatric kewpie-doll, his imaged self
made real—*I didn't ask to be the way I am,*
sobbing now before her understanding
that cannot be surprised by what the night casts up.
Slumped against the cool countertop she
sighs through coffee steam, *Life's funny, isn't it?*
Who'd of thought I'd end up
in this crummy pit-stop! Me, I used to play piano.

They nod in silence with the weight of mystery
under the harsh light,
huddled into their marriage of self-pity.
She sees their doughy choices
reduced to a heap of staling doughnuts
under a plastic dome on a tiered plate.
But never found much comfort in philosophy.

With an attitude resembling love
the woman leans toward him, her mouth
vulnerable beneath the stage-size cupid's bow,
Wanna refill on the house?
So might his mother have addressed him,
no less flirtatiously. Helpless before kindness he
brightens: *Why not, we're only young once!*

She knows this safer language.
That's the speed! We're not dead yet, kiddo!
And ceremoniously fills his cup
with the solemnity of one
extending perfect absolution.

Across the brilliantined asphalt,
counting their dwindled choices and small change,
snuffling derelicts who cannot rent forgiveness
shufflle in expedient contrition
toward the Midnight Mission's neon announcement:
Jesus Saves.

Watching as she retouches her mascara
the Madonna of Alienation
offers her innocent counsel:
I always say life's sad,
but you gotta keep your sense of humour.

Her penitent raises his cup
to toast all things lost in night:
I'll drink to that!

Remembering the many dawns she's seen
struggle for supremacy in the sooty sky
the woman seals the covenant.
Things don't seem so bad in daylight.
Her words float like a benediction
over the incense of coffee.

Amen! exclaims the confessant
his voice constricted with hope
that straddles his tongue,
dry and foreign as a wafer.

Gloating in victory
she crowns the rescue,
anticipates her tip.
Y'want your amen plain or toasted?
Their laughter sputters like bacon
as light masses in fervent efficiency
at the sky's slate edge
to erase the evening's chalky transgressions.

IN MEMORIAM: John Bernard White

1904–1971

The child is the secret essence of its sire.

Arabic proverb

Father, I am your book, you know me well
Yet said so little of this while you lived.
The mysteries that once held you time has sieved
And memory surrenders you to tell
The words that man and boy may rarely say.
I am your inmost essence, your hidden way,
Replication of your heart's deep need;
I voice your silent prayer, retrace your plan
And sorrow for this homeless thing— a man.
My soul's map charts your bravest lonely deed,
Bears imprint of your hope and conquered fears
And love. Shamelessly I shed your unspent tears.
Regard your book— you know to Whom addressed—
And tell blind reader: is the ending blest?

KATHLEEN'S SONG

Life is her cause and love her sole crusade.
She extols, proclaims, upholds them, knows them dear,
Divine and indivisible. Many chilled with fear
Find her warming fire. Service is her simple aid,
Unerring key to recesses of hearts—
She perfects it to a Faith. Her swift joy
And uncunning generosity employ
Her innocence, coax us toward exultancy. Art
And guile are for the wounded— she wields life,
Emits it like halation from which the froward flee.
Her veriest superstitions hold more of truth and glee
Than some religions. How to praise this goodwife,
Earth's God's-penny— all her anonymous kind?
History counts its courtesans and queens. We know it blind.

SONG FOR THOSE NOW SILENT

I shall lie down with my fathers in an auspicious hour,
at the time assigned to this, and they
shall speak soft mossy words
to comfort me in the silent, undiscriminating clay
beyond the song of birds.

Among them I shall find the one I know.
Kate Spottswood of Sligo,
mother of my mother's soul, friend of my youngest days,
and I shall address her, so:
    All your fine sons, Kate,
    all those good men,
      remembered, remembered the length of their days
      your winsome, your wily, your sweet Irish ways.

Ever was she won by love, she who died dancing
in her eighty-sixth year
and went without fear—
the last quilt completed, the loaf baked, peace made—
went to her Lord laughing, as to a lifelong friend,
spent but unbroken at the end.

The potato crop failed. Alone,
not looking back, the girl sailed,
found her own, her one, her splendid man,
gave her goodness, her increase, sinew and bone,
to a new soil. She was not afraid of toil,
of journeys or beginnings.

How was it? she will ask,
and I must say:
  I found it good, Kate, as you found it good,
  the people, the music, the food,
  the towered city, the flowering wood.
For in her facile village way
(who could coax beauty from scraps)
she tutored us to take what came and make it beautiful.
She will dismiss my perilous hesitations, the doubted day;
life was her faith, her innate art, her stay.

How did she implant the impulse to believe?
Stitch it into seams;
dust it with the flour on the crust; weave
or will that tissue in our hearts and heads and dreams;
admit it through the window with the air;
plait it into her strong and lovely daughter's hair;
press it into the white shirts in which she sent her men
to woo and work and worship? Was this the yeast
within the risen cake that marked family festival and holy feast?

It was not by words. She had a subtler way
bred of the peasant: He was simply always there,
the Darling, the Trusted Friend,
and it was pleasant. How did she lend
that faith to us, impress it inexpugnably?
Side with life for it is strong, her actions said,
and if she bent in tears she rose in song.

And did you believe, then? she will bid me relate—
(Humbler of hubris, let this be true!)
  As you showed me, I shall say, acushla, my Kate,
  with lung and liver, limb and loin,
  I had no other way. But knew,
  but knew the Son's redeeméd pledge. The Father came
  and yes, Kate, yes, Oh yes, I knew His Name.

When I am gathered where my fathers now lie dreaming
I shall sing to them about the promised greening.

UNFINISHED BUSINESS

*I have come to the realization that few men fulfil themselves before death,
and I have judged their interrupted work with the more pity.*

Marguerite Yourcenar
Memoirs of Hadrian

Her hair was an improbable shade of magenta and she was
weighted down by unconvincing and aggressively sweeping false
eyelashes, and I adored her on sight. Zalina, or something like it, was
the name she used and indeed she needed no other signature for she
had made the name her own. Even without the embellishments
which included phosphorescent chartreuse eyeshadow she would
have interested me, because her heart was in her face; and at one time
she had been associated with Carol Jane Peters. That is to say, Carole
Lombard. That is to say, Carole Lombard Gable.

I suppose there exists a generation which doesn't know of Marilyn Monroe, let alone Greta Garbo and Carole Lombard, but I cannot concern myself with that. Every age has its Helens who become its metaphors, who symbolize the mysterious essence and glamour of the time, but who appear only curious or quaint or pathetic to subsequent generations. I remember that when I finally saw, in old film clips, Clara Bow, Renee Adoree, Nazimova,[1] Bessie Love and Mary Pickford, who had lighted the fires of admiration in my parents' generation, I wondered what on earth all the fuss had been about, and reflected that the arbiters of beauty of my vitamin-fed sanitized day would have prescribed for Theda Bara several hours under a hot shower and a rigorous slimming programme.

But it is one thing to worship at the altars of the thankfully remote gods and godesses of the entertainment world, and another to become a collector of theatrical celebrities and to indulge in dropping their names casually so that the gleam is dulled and the magic is removed and a name which embodies all the power and excitement of good theatre— say that of Katherine Hepburn, a remarkable actress who enjoys a well-earned reputation— becomes a commonplace. All symbols, all words, must be treated with respect; they wear thin, their evocative capacity diminishes, we grow impoverished of poetry and legends, and the imagination becomes less elastic. We need our living logotypes by which to people our dreams.

Name-dropping is a popular sport which used to flourish, and perhaps still does, with particular intensity in California where some say everything flourishes with particular intensity. The greatest concentration of players was found in that virtual hotbed of the great and near-great, Hollywood, but pockets of enthusiasts of varying degrees of addiction could be found throughout the State. Whatever murky psychological motivations give rise to the need to bolster the self-esteem by engaging in the pastime, it is probably as harmless as hunting and fishing and other forms of trophy-gathering and it is considerably more suited to the non-athletically inclined. As members of this group find their way into the Bahá'í community no

[1] The purpose of this footnote is to express relief that it is not customary in pieces of this kind to include them.

doubt they will attempt to bring their old habits with them, as we all do, but one might hope that name-dropping will not become an extracurricular Bahá'í activity of epidemic proportions, and if isolated instances are observed perhaps it would be desirable to nip them in the bud.

Only once was I ever introduced somewhat irrelevantly to an informal gathering by a friend dedicated to the Bahá'í Cause *and* health foods, as 'Roger White who doesn't like zucchini but who is secretary to Bill Sears' which, if not a disguised exercise in name-dropping whose purpose was to cloak me in borrowed respectability, was perhaps designed to illustrate the extremely tolerant outlook of that distinguished Hand of the Cause whose generosity of viewpoint has always been above reproach and who, in fact, had never expressed the slightest interest in my attitude towards that admirable representative of the vegetable kingdom. Perhaps my chairman's purpose was to place himself squarely on the side of the angels. In any event, I consoled myself with the thought that to be branded publicly as one who snubs zucchini was not quite as shameful as being accused, say, of anti-semitism, and tried to view the matter with a sin-covering eye. I have even succeeded in relating successfully to those of my fellow believers who are devotees of zucchini and are known to consume huge quantities of them. I guess it all comes under the injunction of 'Abdu'l-Bahá that we must avoid circling one another's 'otherness' if we are to achieve unity.[2]

I had little aptitude for the name-game. Of course, I was severely handicapped by the fact that I had once lived in a place called Belleville, Ontario where things were so desperate that aspiring name-droppers had to take refuge in the fact that a few miles farther down the road was Cobourg, birthplace of Marie Dressler. And although in the late 1960s I came to live in California where the Olympics of name-dropping might be said to be held, I didn't settle in the capital of the activity but in a resort community, then still a sleepy smog-free oasis in the California desert where many stars maintained second homes to which they would flee from Los

[2] The purpose of this footnote is to comfort those who don't quite trust a printed page that does not bear them. But in order not to waste it: see *Selections from the Writings of 'Abdu'l-Bahá*, p. 24.

Angeles to rest up from the activities which inspired people to drop their names.

So on my rare weekends in the Hollywood hills with the smart set, listening to them recite with a rehearsed casualness the intimate though innocuous encounters they had at theatre, dinner or cocktail parties with people who were then prominent targets for collectors, and seeing them accumulate conversational high ratings on the equivalent-in-prestige of the Richter scale—five points for Glenda Jackson, for a male, three for a female; the reverse for Robert Redford—I would maintain a discreet silence. That was the better part of wisdom for I had little to contribute.

Of course I was not entirely without resources. I knew Zsa Zsa Gabor's mother's hairdresser. That ought to count for something. Perhaps it would in Belleville. But when you are dealing with big game hunters you can't produce a minnow. The hairdresser was a Bahá'í friend—Andrea Belgreer Funk—and not only was she talented and beautiful and devoted to her deserving husband, but she cooked a marvellous carrot cake which didn't taste the least bit medicinal; one could have one's health and eat one's cake, too, as it were.

And once I met Barbara Stanwyck's maid—or one of them, perhaps—but only because she knew Valerie Mitchell Bourque, another Bahá'í friend, for whom she had much affection and through whom she had developed a sympathy with the Bahá'í teachings; one felt about this attractive and warm-hearted woman that she was in sympathy with all that supported life. Valerie, a charming and accomplished actress, had for some time worked with Miss Stanwyck on her television series *Wagon Train* and still earned royalties from re-runs in compensation for all those hours she had spent staggering along stoically for miles behind a covered wagon through the burning sand wearing a poke bonnet which completely concealed her lovely face. I could get little mileage from my acquaintanceship with Miss Stanwyck's maid, however, since our relationship consisted only of an exchange of names and the next day I couldn't remember hers because I hadn't heard it clearly and had been too timid to ask her to repeat it. I go all to pieces when I'm around those who are around celebrities; but more than that the woman exuded that informal warmth that made one feel one was renewing a friendship rather than beginning to move from the outer fringes of convention toward a hospitable centre.

Such were my meagre accomplishments in the realm of hobnobbing—not a proud record of which to boast, especially when surrounded by champions. I suppose, if pressed, I could admit to having once collided with Kay Ballard in Bullocks. Miss Ballard, though, had little to say on that occasion, possibly because I had severely winded her. In any event she seemed quiet and unassuming by nature and probably would not have welcomed being on the collectors' list. And once I stomped on Molly Berg's foot in a Detroit hotel elevator when she was touring in *A Majority of One* but to speak of it would raise the questions of premeditation and assault on a senior citizen, so I thought it best to keep mum.

But then I met Zalina who might be said to be a name-dropper's name-dropper, and in that sense a celebrity in her own right. She certainly looked as though she might be, in disguise or in decline, someone famous one should know. At a distance and with sympathetic lighting she created the illusion of being a woman of thirty—tall, slender and possessed of that attitude of gaunt hauteur and the facial bone structure once favoured in mannequins before the well-scrubbed and wind-blown look came into fashion and models were suddenly permitted to appear as though they breathed air and knew the light of day. But in fact she was a mite more mature than thirty; say forty years more so. Nevertheless, with her high, sculpted Dietrich-like cheekbones and surgically-assisted face, her seventy-odd springs were at least momentarily belied.

Aiding in the process of challenging the years was a certain calculated wizardry of wardrobe. She had a manner of dressing in eclectic, ambiguous costumes drawn from the *haute couture* of several decades and succeeded in achieving elegance without appearing to be outlandish; she wore snoods, tubans, capes, shawls, scarves and high-necked, long-sleeved tunics of a splendid cut which concealed tell-tale areas of ravage. Seeing her wardrobe was like spending an hour flipping through back issues culled from the archives of *Vogue*.

Zalina's voice was the husky kind which at one time would have been called 'stagey', the kind on which Tallulah Bankhead built her career, and her delivery was pure Amanda in *Private Lives*. No gesture or stance obligatory in silent films and forever made obsolete by method acting and techniques born of subsequent schools was unsuitable to Zalina; she had an entire repertoire of entrances alone. The grand manner might have been her personal invention.

When we met, she had fallen on bitter days and was operating a small, attractive boutique which sold on commission my paintings and decorative items which I handcrafted, often of *papier mâché*. I was treated to Zalina's fascinating monologues always delivered earnestly like a tragedienne's soliloquy, and always revealing. Her head tipped back to draw the jaw line taut, her slim body posed theatrically, hands moving in outsize gestures in a flash of rings, playing the lady down on her luck, she might begin:

'Roger, darling,' (pronounced *dohl-l-l-ing* with a breathy emphasis) 'what am I doing in this tacky little shop? This is not my world. My place is with the beautiful people, the fun people, the people of power and position and prestige. I remember a time when we would rope off several blocks of Hollywood and dance in the street till dawn drinking champagne . . . What has happened to my world, my people?'

Or again:

'The world is changing too quickly for me. What do they want, these angry blacks and these young people in denim with their beards and beads? My world is slipping away . . .'

It was Gloria Swanson's *Sunset Boulevard* come alive. And although her questions were irresistible to a Bahá'í, she did not invite and would not listen to answers, her words seeming to serve primarily a need for self-dramatization. But whatever her theme might be and no matter how tantalizing her hints of a colourful past, the full nature of which she never revealed, eventually, and again in service of her need, she would sprinkle names of importance, liberally, like salt on a tenderloin. 'Lee popped in today just to peek around; Frank asked me over for a drink.' And it was assumed that I would know that she referred to Liberace and Sinatra who owned homes in town. Perhaps her reported encounters were true; I always hoped so. I know that the first of my *objets d'art* she sold was purchased by Liberace, a fact which did much to enhance my status in Zalina's eyes. From that moment I was added to her list of people one telephoned when life at the shop became 'too, too utterly boring.' At any hour of the day or night I might receive a call, usually cryptic, often mysterious. My favourite consisted of Zalina's one sentence— 'Roger, darling, I feel a hot pink mood coming on, distinctly hot pink; tomorrow you *must* bring in some clever something you've made in hot pink'—and she replaced the receiver before I could ask for suggestions or protest.

Her past remains a mystery, though I was given episodic glimpses. She appears to have been at one time or another more or less respectably involved in editing a fashion magazine, in designing clothes, in beauty counselling, and engaged in various capacities in the world of dance and theatre and films. I would have despaired of ever being more than an audience to her rambling recitals were it not for the fact that during one of her discursive tours of the past she dropped a name which rang like crystal: Carole.

'Do you mean Carole Lombard?'

Zalina fixed me with a glance that would not have been out of place on the face of Sir John Gielgud if an imprudent member of an opening-night audience interrupted a *Hamlet* soliloquy to ask who wrote the lines.

'What do *you* know of Miss Lombard?' Her manner was hostile; I was in danger of trespassing on something personal.

I confessed to a lifelong admiration for Miss Lombard's work in films and spoke of feeling for her a spiritual bond, then paused wondering whether to say more. I was prevented from continuing by the expression on Zalina's face. I had won points. The atmosphere was charged suddenly with a lightness, an elation. I wondered whether from the Kingdom of Light this was not a guided experience, some unfinished business in which I was an unwitting agent.

Zalina's mask dropped, layers of affectation and studied mannerisms peeled away, and I was facing another Zalina. Here was the frightened, lonely old woman, the child of God. These thresholds are to be crossed with reverence. For the first time since I had met her she spoke in what must have been her normal voice. A sense of awe flooded me.

'Roger,' she said, and I noticed with gratitude that the traditional 'darling' was dispensed with, 'let me tell you about Carole Lombard. I was her dresser; I designed many of her clothes. She was the most wonderful human being I ever knew and I loved her.'

Now there were tears in Zalina's eyes and an even greater sincerity in her tone.

'Let me say what I have never told anyone. I have never known what people mean when they speak about God or the soul; those words mean nothing to me, I am not a religious woman. I have never prayed. I don't know what it is like to be able to pray. But whatever I know of the sense of any of those words, I know because of Carole Lombard. How can I say it? She was so vital, so alive, so intelligent; she was like quicksilver. There was something about her spirit that I never saw in anyone else. She was lit up from within as though she drew light from an invisible source. She is beautiful in her photographs, but they don't capture that radiance, and no one else I ever met had it.'

'Then you must have been affected by her tragic death?'

'I have never been able to accept her death; I refuse to believe she is dead. Don't misunderstand—I'm not interested in psychic experiences or the occult, it isn't that. But when I wake up in the morning I invariably call her name aloud, I talk to her, like a silly old fool. I say 'Carole, help me through this day! Carole, wherever you are, reach out and help me.' Just saying her name gives me comfort, I feel assisted. Is that prayer? Is that the kind of thing people mean when they say they feel drawn closer to the world of God? If that's what it is, then it's because of Carole. Oh, if you could have known her! If you could have seen her vitality, her fierce love of truth, her hatred of the phoney and the sham. Not everyone saw it; they were distracted by her beauty and wit. She'll be maligned, and has been. People write of her abrasive manner and abusive speech—it was as though she were trying to bludgeon people into being truthful, and she was always surrounded in the entertainment industry by the fake. I never saw such a drive for truth, such a radiance of spirit, in anyone; and few saw it for what it was. Gable— poor conventional, conservative, square, structured Gable—he saw it. He was earthbound, she was airborne. When she entered his life it was like sunlight moving across the face of a mountain. He was dazzled by her spirit.'

And so I was able eventually to speak to Zalina about 'Abdu'l-Bahá and present her with a prayer book, suggesting that whether she addressed God or that realm of radiance to which she felt her friend had taken flight, she would find comfort in the words, particularly knowing that Miss Lombard had herself used them, that possibly these were the source of her mercurial energy and illumination. If Miss Lombard had ever presented the message of Bahá'u'lláh to her, Zalina had no recollection of it, she said, but 'Yes, yes, I want to learn how to pray; I want to use these words.'

It was interesting to me that though Zalina claimed casual possession of the friendship of many celebrities, she did not suggest that she had been an intimate of Miss Lombard, as though she recognized that we are rarely as close to those we admire as our desire to be persuades us that we are.

I saw her only a few times after that before I left California and each time we met we started at some trivial point; one always returns to the beginning. Although there was now a qualitative difference in our relationship, the pattern of theatricality was always repeated, the monologues continued. But any time I would ask questions about Carole Lombard I was given access immediately to another side of Zalina. The prayers helped, she said; she felt solaced and drawn closer to Miss Lombard. And Zalina paid me a great compliment, in words that could not have come easily to her. We rarely speak from our inner worlds.

'The kindest man I ever knew was Stan Laurel of the Laurel and Hardy team and you remind me of him; I mean, not only are you skinny like he was, but you're, well, kind . . .'

One halting sentence, the left-handedness of which would not have escaped my Irish grandmother's notice, but it was addressed from the heart. I could imagine that I heard Miss Lombard giggle with delight.

My own sense of theatre would prefer the glib ending. I would have chosen to have had Zalina, with Hollywood presto-chango flair, embrace the Bahá'í Cause with fervour, give up her worldly ways and go pioneering to some remote outpost where she would live in a maximum of physical discomfort—malaria, of course, a pestilential climate, and man-eating crocodiles. It is not given us to hand-pick the miracles we are privileged to witness, to choose the hungry we are privileged to feed, to select the empty-handed who cross our path. Our instruction is to offer freely the sweet cup; the recipient may sip, or drain it dry. I had no expectation, nor had I the right to hold expectation, that Zalina would become a Bahá'í in any administrative sense; she expressed no interest in the Faith beyond the prayers. 'Carole had *joy*. I want to know that joy,' she said.

Was it enough that Zalina had been led (by *what?* by *whom?*) to the means of the enkindlement of the soul, to the Greatest of Names? As we move laboriously towards wisdom we learn to leave these questions to the scattering angels. The censorious, arrogant mind which leaps so spryly to the bidding of the ego has quite enough to occupy its time.

Whatever the future held, our last conversation indicated that Zalina's feet were still planted firmly on familiar paths. She told me about her new 'gentleman acquaintance', the old-fashioned phrase not seeming incongruous on her lips despite her description of him in the next breath as 'something of a swinger' which was then a popular vulgarity. They had dined and danced and he had, she considered, proved himself unusually perceptive. When he asked her if she would accept a memento of their first meeting she had told him she was a sentimental girl who appreciated flowers, perfume and candy. 'Even my closest friends have difficulty selecting more *personal* gifts for me because I have singularly individual taste,' she'd told him.

'He understood perfectly, Roger! With the long-stemmed roses came a nice little cheque for $350.'

Nor was that all. There were further trysts, the romance flowered.

'Now he wants me to accept a somewhat more permanent token of his affection and has asked me what I might like.'

I was savouring 'token of his affection' but I was all ears.

'I've thought and thought about it, and finally I've decided.'

'Well, Zalina?' The exaggerated pause had been my cue.

'Roger, something *secure*. Perhaps a small condominium . . .'

I never saw my spunky, incorrigible friend again. But observe—I name her as it is human wont to do. *Kind*, she generously named me; *courageous,* I name her; for we pay homage to attributes in the diviner exercise of our need to name.

And what name shall we give that bright spirit whose impact, even after the passage of more than a quarter century, was Zalina's tenuous yet tenacious lifeline to the imperishable realm of laughter, of light, of ceaseless rejoicing?

I beg of God that ye will be bringers of joy, even as are the angels in Heaven.

. . . Wherefore, O ye Bahá'ís, strive ye with all your might to create, through the power of the Word of God, genuine love, spiritual communion and durable bonds among individuals. This is your task.

'Abdu'l-Bahá

THE REPROACH

The hour you asked for
to say goodbye
has stretched to six,
and still you sit
passively accepting
the tattered ends
of my frayed hospitality,
expertly polishing your poised smile
to a glistening bow of reproach.
Only as you disappointedly savage
the paper napkin
do I see that you await,
as you have always awaited,
the perfect rejection.
Your self-assessment, of course,
is your concern,
but now that you present it to me
for tacit confirmation
I know what I must do.
Soon I shall offer you
another cup of tea;
soon say: Has it occurred to you, my dear,
that God accepts you?

STATELESS PERSON

Her name has been a valid passport
admitting him to capitals she conquered
where her memory is banked coin.

His voice is encroachingly intimate,
the smile that of an ambassador
from the hushed sleek towers
of a necessitous kingdom
where no traffic hums
nor sovereign reigns.
With the professional handshake,
the oiled hinge of 'I believe you know my wife . . .'
The desolate eyes simulate warmth.
'. . . she's a very special person.'

Persuasively pitched
the voice petitions entry.
We would rush to give him
freedom of the city but the terms are clear.
Cast her out, he silently solicits,
agree she was my ruin.
Orphaned from self
he stands at our gate whining,
his pockets chinking with a copious rage
which we may borrow.

The unbribable heart in heated debate
struggles to confer citizenship
knowing his documents forged.

'Issue a visa', compassion argues cogently,
'negotiate terms of residence later.'

We advance smiling.
'Yes, a very special person.'

MATINÉE FOR ONE

Saichiro Fujita: A Reminiscence
(1886–1976)

I never felt that I could do very much for 'Abdu'l-Bahá.
One thing I did was perhaps acceptable—sometimes I made Him laugh.

Fujita

We called him 'Fudge' but the confection which bears that name does not describe Fujita; he was rather more like one of those delectable and mysterious sauces, piquant and puzzlingly subtle, that linger on the tongue surprising the taste-buds with delightful and unexpected combinations of unsuspected ingredients—the under-taste of brown sugar, the hint of cinnamon, the startling sting of lemon. Fujita met the need of the human taste for delighted astonishment: his flavour was 'maverick' in perfect balance with 'fidelity.' Without the condiments represented in his character the salad of unity in diversity would be bland fare indeed.

The faithful and much loved servant, in turn, of 'Abdu'l-Bahá, Shoghi Effendi and the Universal House of Justice, Fujita remained very much his own man. Unfailingly courteous and dignified in his dealings with everyone, he admitted one to friendship slowly. Usually only after a few astringent skirmishes, designed to weed out those he labelled as 'stuffed shirts,' 'pompous busy-bodies' and 'smart guys in awe of their education,' did he lower the bridge across the wide moat that protected his privacy. The seen and the invisible worlds were interfluent in Fujita. He moved between them with the natural ease that is frequent in children and the fey, inevitable in the sensitive during a peak experience, and intrinsic to the genius and the truly spiritual. He was possessed of keen intelligence and brilliant wit and that rarest of gifts, the wisdom to use them well. His speech was terse and epigrammatic. He could exasperate, delight and entertain in quick succession, but no one seemed able to resist him. To the end of his life he remained accessible to those who sought him out, for he recognized the need of the Bahá'ís to make contact with him as a link with the period of the Ministry of 'Abdu'l-Bahá, and he succeeded in doing so without surrendering his jealously-guarded privacy.

As often must be done by those with a tremendous capacity for attraction, Fujita perfected evasion to an art. The bore, the pedant, the obtuse, the fake, soon saw him slip from their grasp. The luckless intruder who blundered uninvited with tactless questions into his personal sphere, and the zealous and tyrannical missionary who sought to impose upon him some well-intentioned catechism of self-improvement, were soon left to their own resources—he would skitter off, pretending not to hear, humming to himself, possibly blowing them kisses and performing a soft-shoe dance or some act of buffoonery at which no one could take the slightest offence. 'He's always so very much *himself!*' was a remark often made of him. And if an appropriate reply might have been 'Yes, impossible!' one did not hear it spoken. One almost wished it were possible for him to conduct courses on How to Grow Old and Remain Engaging, but part of his charm was that the thought would not have occurred to him. He took no advantage of being a celebrity and felt under no obligation to reform or impress his fellow Bahá'ís, yet few were unconscious in meeting him that his was the beard that 'Abdu'l-Bahá had playfully tweaked.

Each encounter with Fujita yielded up treasure. Consider this nugget of nonagenarian wit: Fujita lamented to Ethel Crawford that he was beginning to experience the physical limitations of age and that he felt he needed a nurse to look after him. 'But nurses are so expensive,' Ethel replied, wary of a trap. 'I didn't say I was going to pay her; I just said I needed her!' was Fujita's rejoinder, accompanied by a wink and a chuckle. He had, indeed, remarkably clear ideas about what is appropriate to a full life. Once, in his late eighties, after an illness, he was directed to recuperate in a rest home which offered medical care. He made an accelerated return to convalesce in his own cottage, on the grounds of the Master's house, complaining that he had not been happy at the rest home. 'It was full of *old* people,' he protested.

Once I came upon him as he sat cross-legged on the walk in the garden at No. 10 Persian Street, hugging to his chest the copy of *The Bahá'í World*, vol. XIV, he had just received. Tears were streaming down his face. He looked up from the 'In Memoriam' section in which he had been engrossed. 'Look! Kathryn Frankland! She told me about Bahá'u'lláh and 'Abdu'l-Bahá in 1903! And here's the story of how she met me. She called me 'the little squirrel!''

'And now she's with 'Abdu'l-Bahá,' I commented somewhat lamely, for I had not seen Fujita in tears before and was half wondering why the experience should seem so natural and free from embarrassment. Fujita lived for the most part in an inner landscape where the Master strode with a light free step, His robe lifting in the wind, His boyish laughter ringing behind Him—sentimentality had no place in that inscape. I watched Fujita weigh my remark for spurious content; he would dismiss it if it were counterfeit. I felt relief when I earned his warm grin. 'Yeah,' he said, 'she beat me to it!' He stood up, dusted himself off and ambled away with his Chaplinesque ragdoll gait, looking smaller and more vulnerable than ever. He was conscious of his size, but accepting of it; he had a *tall* dignity. Only the foolhardy, oblivious to peril, patronized him.

One could not have known 'Abdu'l-Bahá and Shoghi Effendi without reflecting whether one might have unwittingly added to their burdens, caused them grief. Whatever difficulties Fujita caused, or imagined he caused, were probably redeemed in part by his ability to create laughter in their lives. The notes of early pilgrims attest his capacity to bring smiles to the lips of the Master. In the Persian Bayán (VII, 18) the Báb extols the 'nearness to God' of those 'who bring joy to the hearts of the believers.' Fujita was a superlative actor; those who saw it will not forget his impersonation of a camera-happy tourist staggering about with his eye glued to an imaginary viewfinder, emitting loud clicks. He showed affection through unobtrusive kindnesses and was an inveterate tease. One frequently saw him lugging a basket laden with fruits and flowers, gifts for his friends. It was not unusual for one of the ladies serving in the Holy Land to be presented with lemons accompanied by his wistful hint, 'Did I ever tell you that lemon pie is my favourite?' Who could fail to succumb to such an outrageous stratagem? A few days later Fujita's benefactress would receive a charming and formal written note which might say: 'That was the best *apple* pie I ever tasted.' And sometimes one was treated to a more elaborate jest.

I was enjoying the luxuriant shade of a bougainvillaea in the garden at the temporary seat of the Universal House of Justice one warm afternoon in the summer of 1975. Obscured, I thought, from Fujita's view by the overhanging bush, I saw him leave the building with his spry and springing step. He carried on his shoulder a large cardboard carton—obviously empty from the ease with which he hoisted it—and was intent on one of those industrious errands with which he occupied himself. His face, as elegant and inscrutable as that of a figure carved in ivory by the hand of an oriental master, contrasted curiously with the scuffed tennis shoes and the frayed blue jeans which would have fit a slight eleven year old boy—but whatever his costume, Fujita was always cloaked in a private dignity, and as irresistible as the image evoked by the juxtaposition of the words 'Japanese/Leprechaun.'

Half-way down the walk he paused, his expression thoughtful, and placed the empty carton on the paving. Then an energetic pantomime ensued: adjusting the position of the box, stepping back to examine it, registering satisfaction, and then with amazing agility leaping into the box and scrunching down with an expression of utter bliss. I might have guessed the rest—the turning on of invisible taps, the lathering of unseen soap, the impersonation of the bathroom amateur baritone warming up, Fujita's emergence from the box, the elaborate drying off with an invisible towel, the emptying of the imaginary water. Marcel Marceau could not have equalled the performance. Then placing the box upon his shoulder, Fujita proceeded on with an expression of serene innocence as though nothing untoward had occurred, until he reached the shrub from behind which I had in amused astonishment, and I thought undetected, observed the spectacle, part surreal, part music-hall turn. His voice appeared to be addressed to the bougainvillaea: 'Young man, if you're going to spy on me, I'm going to make it worth your while!' And off he scampered, chuckling heartily.

I'm still mining that performance for nuances, for instruction, for its wealth of pure fun. I don't believe it was Fujita's purpose merely to prove me a failed spy and himself a prankful old man; nor solely to educate me in the privileges of age and the prerogatives of privacy; nor entirely to admonish the spectre of self-righteousness that lingers in each of us to stifle our capacity for joy, to cause us to shrink from the challenge of the absurd and capricious, to blind us to the mystery and miracle. Fujita had seen me scribbling in notebooks and drawn his own uninnocent conclusions:

You knew I'd preserve this, didn't you, Fudge?

PART SIX:

SALT LICK

Satire is never wasted on trivia.

David Loth

No one is exempt from talking nonsense: the misfortune is to do it solemnly.

Philip Howard

PSALM FROM AN EAST LONDON PUB

Book wanted: 'The History and Social Influence of the Potato' by R. N. Salaman. Box No. 20001.

Advt. in *The Bookseller*
18 November 1978

Well, just think about it, 'erbie,
all them grubby shopgirls and lonely sailors
strolling around Brighton, say,
casually munching their greasy chips.
And all across America
in 'undreds of 'oward Johnsons
them squalid travelling men, rumpled tourists
and road-weary families with their mewling brats
tucking into their fries
with never a thought for the potato's pedigree,
to say nothing of its 'istory and social influence.
It's a rum picture that. Ungrateful lot!

Makes you think
the 'uman race deserves whatever befalls it—
all them wars and revolutions and disasters.
I mean to say, like,
if people will take the potato for granted
wot many of them eats every day,
'ow do they feel about God?

Oh, I guess 'e loves the world, all right,
seeing as 'ow 'e created it,
but irregardless,
being taken for granted just won't wash with 'im forever.
There'll be a day of reckoning, mark my words.

I tell you, mate, it don't 'alf 'ave me worried . . .

A TABLED QUESTION

One word frees us of all the weight and pain of life:
That word is love.

Sophocles
Oedipus at Colonus, l. 1616

(Lines to be spoken at breakneck speed while holding a hot potato in the mouth, and in the manner one might suppose would be adopted by one bearing the name Brenda Beastley-Fawndler.)

Do I love you? What an extraordinary question! I mean, Basil dear, when one sits down to tea and has just reached for an utterly delicious-looking watercress sandwich, one isn't quite prepared to have one's husband come lunging into the room demanding to know in that urgent tone of voice whether one loves him. It's all so startling. I'm not even sure whether it's the sort of conversation one should have over tea—I can't imagine that it aids digestion. Now don't say another word, darling, there's no need to look apologetic—I can see from your face that the question has some importance for you and I wish to answer it in a way that will satisfy you. Milk or lemon, darling?

Now let me see whether I grasped your meaning: you asked me—and, darling, as you did so your eyes were bulging in a most ludicrous way—you said—I think these are your exact words, they rather impressed themselves on my mind because of their unusual nature to say nothing of the rather melodramatic tone in which you addressed me—your precise words were 'Brenda, do you love me?' Darling, do stop stirring your tea in that absent-minded manner—I find it impossibly distracting and I really do wish to give the most serious consideration to your, shall we say, bizarre question—or is that too strong a word?—an out-of-the-ordinary question, certainly. I can't think what might have prompted it. Perhaps you have had an especially difficult day at the bank? Or no, perhaps instead you're remembering that next week is our wedding anniversary? Dearest, do stop toying with the sugar tongs—it quite destroys my train of thought.

'Brenda, do you love me?' you said. Well darling, I suppose the simple truth is I've never thought about it. I mean to say, is it the sort of thing one needs to think about? After all, I married you and I've borne your children and managed your home—created a home for you and managed it, I suppose, to put it more accurately—and I should suppose one could infer from those circumstances that I entertain affection for you—it might be seen as prima facie evidence of a degree of sympathetic interest in you, as my father would be inclined to say when adopting his most judicial manner, his most 'Queen's Counsel' air.

Dearest, don't fidget so—I want to think about your question and give you an answer that will make you happy. And your happiness has always meant everything to me—more evidence, one might suppose, of the fact of my—well, caring considerably for you. I'm not suggesting, dear, that affording you an exalted place in my affections is a difficult thing to do—you are quite the kindest man—well, perhaps excepting papa—quite the kindest man I've ever known. You've always been very generous to me and—well, kind. And patient, too, with my strange little ways. I don't suggest for an instant that my behaviour has always been such as to not call upon your reserve of patience. I'm certainly very fond of you—I quite like you, in fact—and I'm sure the children do too, although I confess it hasn't occurred to me to ask them about it. I mean, it's not the sort of question one thinks to put to oneself let alone the children who have quite all they can manage with cramming for their O levels and their struggling with French lessons and adjusting to their utterly unsympathetic tennis instructor. But if I may venture to speak for them—and as their mother surely this is a right I may momentarily arrogate—is that the word I want? I mean a right I may claim if only briefly—if I may speak for the children I would say I am certain they find you very agreeable. Oh I'm sure they do. I'm positive they find you kind and generous and patient. In fact, I suppose if I stop to think of it even your question—ill-considered as it was and just blurted out in that totally unexpected way—your question might be seen as another expression of your kindness—yes, I can quite clearly see it in that light, with just the tiniest effort.

It is really most kind of you to want to know whether I hold you in esteem. A less sensitive man— oh it becomes clearer as I think about it— one less delicate, less attuned to nuances, wouldn't be the least concerned about how his wife felt about him. Yes, yes I do see it now and, darling, it was so utterly kind of you to put the question— I should have seen it at once, your kindness, I mean. You might have found a more felicitous way of expressing it, of course, but on reflection I think I understand what you meant when you asked 'Brenda, do you love me?' How extraordinarily kind! It's rather like asking 'Is your mattress lumpy?' or 'Do you prefer jam or marmalade with your toast?' The sort of thing one says to express total concern for another's well-being— when one wishes to establish an unusual degree of intimacy in communication.

How utterly precious of you to ask me whether I love you! Darling, do let me think about it for a while and find a way of answering that will make you happy. It's not the sort of answer one just plunges into the way they do in novels and films. 'Brenda, do you love me?' It would, I suppose, depend on one's definition of love. Tell you what, dear, do let me think about it some more and I promise I shall give you an answer soon. Basil, dear, you have such a vacant expression in your eyes— whatever are you thinking about? Have you heard a word I've said? You really are in a most extraordinary mood today. I sometimes wonder, dearest, whether you really love me.

JINGLE

On reading the poems of yet another barefoot boy and finding not much to admire except the royalties.

I, the happy wanderer, now old and stiff of joint,
Took my little pencil out and licked its tiny point.

I, the carefree vagabond, friend of elves and gnomes,
Sat upon a toadstool and wrote some charming poems.

I, the barefoot traveller, though growing bald and bored,
Write of brooks and shady nooks and country lanes explored.

I, the vagrant gipsy, though I've lumbago now,
With zest told of my airy quest—not the why, the how.

I, the bard of by-ways wrote, though rheumy in the eye,
Of effervescence, adolesence, me, myself, and I.

I, the lissom laddie wrote, though aged and choked with phlegm,
Of princes, kings and fairy rings and spoke quite well of them.

I, the weary wafter, now somewhat short of breath,
Wrote with zeal of all that's real, excluding life and death.

I, the maundering minstrel, use words sweet as cream buns.
I've a Muse I'd not abuse by choosing naughty ones.

I, the well-known wayside imp, with geriatric flair,
Wrote verse that's pure and won't endure—my banker doesn't
care.

I, the senile drifter, the former merry boy,
Wrote a hundred darling poems. $\phi\theta\varepsilon V$! how they cloy!

THE MINIMAL MINIMALIST POEM

'I love you.' How's that?
    Well, you're getting close . . .
Add: 'Very much.' Quite pat!
    Darling, too verbose.
More minimal, then: 'Love.'
Totally clear?
    Admirably terse.
    But what does 'love' *mean,* dear?
Oh, go write your own minimal verse!

ON FIRST LOOKING INTO
BARTLETT'S FAMILIAR QUOTATIONS

The bards have all addressed you, Death,
Care you to hear from me?
I well may choose to snub you
Throughout eternity.

You have heard the great ones speak—
I might blush and stammer
Adding to your other chores
Correction of my grammar.

HOT LINE

The first intimation one receives of a poem is like listening to a long distance telephone call on a bad line.

George Barker

All right, I'll read it back or have no sleep.
Don't call when I'm in bed, won't this thing keep?
Of course I'm cross. Lately I've been thinking
You only call when destitute or drinking.

Love's urgent claim is feathered and emphatic . . .
The next was lost, I couldn't hear for static
Or else you dropped your voice. *Clawed?* Well, okay.
Clawed, it soars above our— something—*day* . . .

I didn't sneeze. For heaven's sake don't cry!
An adjective is easy to supply.
I missed the next as well, just heard a beep.
Is this a call-box? Why disturb my sleep . . .

Inattentive? What a rotten thing to say—
You call me late and drive my wife away . . .
The jealous type, and how can I explain
These hot-breath calls? Why shouldn't I complain . . .

. . . oh, let's get on: *To strike the small furred
heart,* I think you said— you rather slurred—
Oh yes you did! . . . *to bear it high*— this bit's unclear—
Too terrorized to understand its fear . . .

And that was it. Then you started fighting,
I suppose you think those four lines are exciting?
A little trite, old girl: 'love seen as bird',
But then you always were romantic and absurd.

Satisfied? Call back when I'm alone;
My wife is asking who is on the phone.
Here's a kiss! I'm hanging up— goodbye!
And don't go ringing up some other guy.

FOR MEN ONLY

Traditionally a male literary critic feels that he can heap no higher
praise upon a female author than to say she writes like a man; his
greatest scorn of a male writer consists of saying he writes like a
woman.
'. . . *There must always be two literatures, like two public toilets, one for
Men and one for Women. Sometimes it seems that no achievement can
override this division* [*established by literary criticism*].'

Mary Ellman
Thinking About Women

This is a he-male-poet's poem,
lean and muscular, horrendously hirsute
masterful as a pneumatic drill,
nothing limp and lavender about it,
no secondary sexual characteristics
in this achieving son-of-a-sestina.

Look! Direct, forceful, to the point—
scarcely into the first stanza
and already using dirty words: *sextain*.

Observe the manly way it swaggers down the page,
the butch adjectives bulging like biceps.
Even the alliteration is athletic.
Moves onomatopoeically, too:
    clang/clank/clink/clonk/clunk.
No pantywaist pussyfooter, this one.
As for women, likes them floccus,
with a touch of phonaesthesia:
    flap/flick/flirt/flit/flounce/fluff/flutter.

This poem will never cry.
Lisping editors quail before its assertive manner,
dropping their effete eyeshades,
their swish blue pencils.
Note the decisive placement of the taut commas,
the virile authority of this full stop ☞ .

Gets lonely sometimes, though;
has already thought
of taking a want-ad in the Personals:
    Attractive free masculine meter
    interested in intimate polarisation
    with cultured, curvacious sonnet.
    Object: couplets.

Rumour has it that the gentleman prefers blondes;
that only pinkfrilly stereotypes
will be considered;
that his objective was always objects.

PRAYER FOR PROTECTION

I'm not sure why I cannot accept . . . at the base of the poems is a good deal of talent. It seems odd to say, with a non-acceptance, but there's something in the poems that tends toward greatness . . . the language? I don't know . . .

> (letter of rejection from an editor received by a friend in response to poems with a spiritual theme)

The impulse toward excellence persists, despite well-intentioned agencies, and so does the desire for it.

D. J

O God, we beg of Thee to inure us
to the shoddy and the second-rate
that we be not challenged by perfection,
for excellence is Thine alone
and we seek no giddy visions.

Increase, O Lord, our ardour for the awful
and the odiously ordinary;
endear to us the enduring dreadful
and purify our desires
that we may covet naught save kitsch.

Fill our ears with jingles and the Top Ten Tunes;
place before our modest gaze drab daubs
and no graven images save calendar cheesecake
that we may magnify the mediocre unto the multitude.

In Thy mercy, withhold not from us any tinkling triviality.
Spread before us a bountiful banquet of banality
that our hearts may be kept humble
and our souls find tranquil rest.

Strengthen our resolve to accept with meekness
immeasurable mundanity and meretriciousness
that we may not lust for literature,
ache for art, or hunger after heaven.

Allot to us, O munificent Lord, only that
which is mendacious, mercenary and unmemorable,
for we aspire to be numbered among
Thy worthy servants who live easefully on Thine earth.

Deliver us from all that tends toward greatness
that we may feast upon the fleeting and the false
and if it be within Thy power
protect us forever from the knowledge
of why we raise this prayer.

ASTERISK POEM

*Reach out and comfort me, beloved, for I am frail and human and
alone, and death awaits me.*

I hope you found the potroast tender, dear,
She said, darting him a furtive anxious look
meaning perhaps among other things *————————————
———

and *Soothe my fears, assure me I am adequate.*
He grunted uncomprehendingly from behind his book.
So went their years. She left when his affairs and drinking
    forced her.
She never talks to me, he told the Court the day that he divorced her.

The rosebed I planted is doing well, he said,
meaning perhaps among other things * —————————————
———

and *Assure me I am adequate, though weak—when young*
    I sometimes cried.
But she, surveying the merciless handiwork of time and calories
shown by her mirror merely bit her lip and sighed.
Lonely and insecure she took to nagging as a cover.
He never talks to me, she told her friend the day she took a lover.

AN OFF-DAY AT THE POEM FACTORY

. . . occasionally a writer becomes obsessed by the sonnet form. Merrill Moore
wrote at least one sonnet a day for most of his adult life, winding up with so
many thousands of them that the reader is discouraged even before he begins
reading any of them . . . he wrote nothing but sonnets, a preoccupation that
cannot fail to seem excessive.

Frances Stillman

It's time to write the Sonnet-of-the-Day,
Four hundred is my quota for this year;
What should the subject be? I'm not too clear—
I'm frankly running out of things to say.
(I write of Love and Death and shed a tear,
Daunting readers by prolixity, I fear.)
Perhaps to open: *How do I love thee . . .*
No, someone wrote that line— could it be me?
As each thought comes I wonder if I read it,
If Shakespeare, Milton, Donne or Shelley said it,
Or Emily D., or Edgar Allan Poe . . .
(This is the twelfth, just two more lines to go!)
The best of bards I'd be, how well I know it,
Were industry the measure of a poet.
I've lost my rhyme scheme now I think upon it.
Line sixteen—*Oh damn, I've spoiled the sonnet!*

LO! HOW HIS MUSE DOTH HIM ABUSE

Those who have been brought up on Romantic poetry tend to think that all poets ought to find inspiration in the beauties of the countryside, and are inclined to dismiss as unhealthy or as morally suspect those who look elsewhere for the experiences that set in motion the poetic faculty.

John Press
The Fire and the Fountain

Rustic cottage, flowered dell,
Suited ancient poets well.
The muse of Shelley, Keats and Milton
Sang not at the Conrad-Hilton.

Wooded glen and singing lark
Struck those bards' creative spark.
My jaded muse refrains from humming
Until assured of indoor plumbing.

Surely all great odes must be
Inspired by muse on sun-kissed lea?
Mine could linger there an aeon
And pine for penthouse, Rolls-Royce, neon.

My muse only favours me
At Harrods, Saks or Tiffany;
Shuns babbling brook and bower shady—
A most sophisticated lady.

The lady scorns the nymph and faun,
Prefers, instead, Pierre Cardin.
No nods or becks or wreathèd smiles
Till gambolling in Gucci's aisles.

Confined to garret or quaint cellar
My muse longs for Bonwit-Teller.
When Neiman-Marcus is her goal,
With rapturous song she fills my soul.

I think I shall be slow to see
My verses in anthology.
I'd be immortal somewhat quicker
Were not my muse a city-slicker.

REPLY IN KIND

I'm troubled, I'm dissatisfied, I'm Irish.

Marianne Moore
Spenser's Ireland

Shall we take refuge in being Irish
   as does Miss Moore
Or courageously search for
   an explanation less obscure?
Should we maintain that having ties
   with the old sod
Guarantees our having trouble
   with our whiskey and our women
   and our God?
The old order changeth,
   yielding place to new
Said Tennyson, and despite his being English
   might this not be true?
The Irish hold no monopoly on dissatisfaction;
   do you ask proof?
Malcontent today comes in all flavours—
   even Alacaluf.

May we not retreat from the ambiguity
  of Miss Moore's position
And assert that spiritual unrest is now
  universally the human condition?
Some hold that the Prophets foretold
  what was coming
And made it abundantly clear that the source
  of current disturbances
  is somewhat more profound than lack
  of the equal distribution of wealth
  and of indoor plumbing.
Scratch any Irishman
  and beneath his querulous complaint
You are likely to find
  (well buried under layers of
  sentimentality and irascibility)
  a budding saint
And in or out of his cups
  and on or off the dole
Most are prepared to concede that all men's troubles
  are rooted in the soul.

WELL MIGHT YOU ASK, MR FROMM, MAY MAN PREVAIL?

If God has died
And Christ has lied
And science has burst faith's bubble,
Yet none descry
The twice-starred sky—
M'lads, there may be trouble.

LUNCH COUNTER: WOOLWORTH'S

The adjustment would be simple:
add a cameo, perhaps,
a touch of écru lace;

Approve the regal bearing,
the silver hair, the cup rim's
lack of lipstick trace;

Subtract the chrome and clatter
and we behold the elegant grandame
with 18th century drawingroom grace;

But no charity of imagination
can annul the slithering, wobbling hotdog,
the mustard on her face.

O sweet irony!
O sweet American dream!

HIAWATHA REVISITED

*If one more liberal white visitor to the Yukon tells me I am a noble savage I
may take a tomahawk and demonstrate just how noble I really am.*
(remark by a Tlingit friend)

It is the redskin's noble task
To be someone's invention,
The face fixed in a stony mask,
The *Ugh* and *How* convention;

A stoic who does not know fear,
Sleek, neatly-plaited hair,
A name to please the paleface ear—
Lone-Dog or Bee-Bites-Bear;

The loincloth fickle in a breeze,
Bead necklaces that throttle,
Feathers wont to make one sneeze,
A weakness for the bottle;

Forecasting weather on request,
Striking savage poses,
To always ride or paddle West's
Less fun than one supposes;

Telling time by phase of moon,
Remembering to be lazy,
To grunt and stalk and skulk quite soon
Can drive a fellow crazy;

The movies one must suffer through
Learning what's required!
Like Tonto say *Heap big* and you
Are thought to be inspired.

But never to be truly seen
Or known to think or feel;
To fall between two worlds and scream
Unheard— where films are real.

'IF YOU'RE GOING
TO TALK WATERMELON, PRISSY,
THEN DON'T Y'ALL TALK
WITH YOUR MOUTH FULL' . . .

That's what I tell that shiftless child
every time she comes shambling in
to report in coloratura some small catastrophe
in the kitchen. She has a taste for doom.

Lawsy, Mizz Scawlet, she says, on the edge of hysteria,
dis here ole' plantation is in big trouble . . .

Always *Mizz Scawlet* this and *Mizz Scawlet* that!
Why, a body would go mad if she listened.
Land sakes! I sometimes have a mind to have Rhett
give her a good thrashing—
it might improve her diction, if not her manners.

Well, bless me, just the other day she waddled in
trailing distress like an ankle chain,
telling me about some li'l ole' bitty thing.
Mizz Scawlet, she whined, *Ahm telling y'all
dere's a big misery heading dis way!
Dose darkies roun' here is mighty restless—
Dey's got a bad case of de jitterin' agitations . . .*

'In that case,' I told her,
'I shall have to think about it tomorrow.'
If I may be forgiven for saying so myself,
I have something of a reputation for serenity and wit.
We like to keep things peaceable here at Tara.

PART SEVEN:

TODDLING TOWARD SALVATION

Humour, in fact, is one of the elements that make up a balanced and complete mentality . . . in that duel between good and evil which the New Testament records, one will find a grave and clear-eyed humour on the side of truth, but none at all in the minds of the Pharisees and Scribes.

George Townshend

Laughter is a token of virtue. No man who has once heartily and wholly laughed can be altogether irreclaimably bad.

Thomas Carlyle

Comedy, laughter, humour seem to me more and more the soul's salvation.

Thomas Mann

CASANOVA, THWARTED

(or with a wary eye upon Christopher Marlowe)

BUT THAT WAS IN
ANOTHER COUNTRY;
AND BESIDES, THE WENCH
WAS A GLUTTON

(which subtitle, though it may mystify the gentle reader, will at least
provide the typesetter employment)

The loving things I long to say
You silence with; 'Have more *pâté?*'

You turn to ash my private wish
By asking: 'Do you like the fish?'

Kisses on your lips I'd lavish,
But find you nibbling on a radish.

I ask that you behold my soul—
Your eyes fix on the salad bowl.

I have no thought for my heaped plate
So sweetly do you masticate.

You turn to me your tender gaze
But ask: 'Please pass the *hollandaise*'.

My wily knee towards yours is pressing.
You baptize it with salad dressing.

I scarce descry my whereabouts,
And you exclaim: 'Such Brussles sprouts!'

I would implore you: 'Be my own!'
But you gnaw on a chicken bone.

Dare I take as love or wife
One so deft with fork and knife?

My hand creeps out with sly intent;
You butter it by accident.

You pity not your helpless thrall
Who loves you, gravy-stains and all.

Would that my thought you might divine;
Instead, you say: 'Do try the wine!'

I sing to you: 'Tra-la! Tra-la!'
But you smile upon the Rum-baba.

You pour my tea, yet give no balm—
Bypass my cup and scald my palm.

As you arise I kiss your nape
And lose a tooth. You peel a grape.

We might, as lovebirds, nestle chirping—
You slump, replete, politely burping.

My deeper need you blithely slight;
Love—not food—my appetite.

Our love is doomed to be platonic—
You interest's plainly gastronomic.

Leaving, I cast a sad glance back—
You fuss about a midnight snack.

Of further trysts make no suggestion.
Sweet dreams be yours. And indigestion.

ENVOI:
Will her virtue heaven win,
If gluttony's her only sin?

OF STATES AND STATESMEN

Kurt Waldheim today warned of the disastrous consequences of a direct confrontation between the world superpowers and stressed that the significance of even regional tensions and conflicts should not be underestimated.

News item
26 January 1980

'Beware the ides of March, Caesar,'
Shakespeare's soothsayer bids
Who today might warn the populace
'Beware the march of Ids.'

THE LEAST

Most of the Bahá'ís in our area are unliterated . . .
(letter from a Bahá'í administrative body)

God makes—you must admit—the strangest choices!
At thought of growing ranks the heart rejoices
But still one asks, quite frankly, why choose *these*?
Why not more B.Sc's and Ph.D's?
He's a tad too democratic for my taste
(Though I'm trying to adjust, I add in haste.)

I suppose by now He knows His business well,
His chosen gladly die for Him—but can they spell?
One is almost led to question His sagacity
In selecting those of such a slight capacity.
In times past with some bedouins (a few)
It's proved amazing, really, what He'll do.
Rome's lions dined on Christians in large masses—
Had martyrs time for literacy classes?
Diplomas were not asked of those brave friends
Who for love, on Persia's soil, met bloody ends.
Devotion's dons aren't always pedagogic
But seem erudite in faith's peculiar logic.
Might God Himself confer His Own degrees
On the learned-in-His-ways—including these?
I concede the call must sound, all raise their voices.
But one must remark He makes the *oddest* choices.
This chilling thought I've often contemplated:
How sorely God does test us *literated*.

A WORD OF WARNING FROM THE WORLD'S YOUNGEST CRABBY OLD MAN

No doubt the aged, and especially the famous aged, are entitled to employ the device of pretended senility and petulance to rid themselves of fools . . .

(letter from a friend)

If the babbling world should thrust me into fame
Do not approach to bask in my acclaim.
I shall be nasty. I'll mispronounce your name.

Do not tilt at me with notebooks when I'm old
Asking silly questions. I'll tell lies and scold
And scorn you. I'll not eat my supper cold.

Do not seek me out pretending amity.
I'll rupture your eardrums and your vanity
With quaint and geriatric profanity.

I'll say *hey-nonny-nonny* and *fiddle-de-dee*
To the snivelling scholar who questions me.
I'll have nothing less than peace when I take tea.

I'll assume entitled privileges of age.
Leonine, thunderous with pungent wind, I'll rage.
You'll think me senile, and blanching flee my cage.

I'll snuffle, burp, abandon niceties
And not conceal my loud and drenching sneeze.
I'll dismay you with my eccentricities.

O! I shall be difficult. I shall not bow
To bores and self-seekers. Shocked, they'll state h
I drove them off. Be warned. I practice even now!

SPORTS

Like Bobby Hull, with speed of flame
I might've scored shots that won the game,
Earned immortality of sorts—
Despite my poems,
Despite my warts.

But riskier was the sport I played
With laurelled victory long delayed—
Perhaps beyond my skill to set
The puck of faith
In heaven's net?

COMMUNICATION

Since speaking is an act of faith
And not a trick of grammar
We may suppose our prayers are heard
Despite our lisp or stammer.

Our head inside a dragon's mouth
In faith's attenuation
Might not our muffled cry still rise—
In heaven find translation?

DIALOGUE

One vision will erect a tent,
Another raise a tower.
Pity that proud unseeing one
Whose scan conceives no bower.

Canvas is but easily rent,
Stones are prone to crumble.
Shelterless I braved the storm.
Might the pious be as humble!

INTERVIEW

I'd thought saints were boring zealots
While the denizens of hell
Might be tolerant and jolly
And like a good time well.

I interviewed a saint or two
And heard no cant or niggling.
When I enquired how they fared
They couldn't speak for giggling.

How does one join this brotherhood?
I thought the answer quaint:
If one thinks *ha ha!*
He's a saint *ho ho!*
He *ha ha! ho ho!* ain't!

SHALOM, etc.

Shalom! I say. Then, as one caught in theft,
Grin sheepishly, of further words bereft.
I agree the language has an ancient heft
But I'm unable to command its warp and weft
So at speaking it I'm frightfully undeft—
Just one gutteral and then my palate's cleft.
How odd to *d.e.a.r.* and *k.a.e.p.s.* from right to left!

THE SELF-CONSCIOUS SATYR

*. . . self-consciousness is a Canadian habit of mind which runs rampant in
our literature . . .*

Joanne Cutt
Quarry-Winter 1979

My love moved through the moonlit glade
As lightly as a fawn
And lingered . . . *er* . . . *um* . . . disarrayed
Until first blush of dawn.

The pearly flesh that I adore
Was soon revealed to me
And I . . . *um* . . . *er* . . . could tell you more
Were I not watching me.

EVERYBODY'S WRITING HAIKU: WHY NOT YOU?

Haiku (also Hokku): Japanese poetic form of 17 syllables arranged in 3 lines of 5, 7 and 5 syllables each.

Britannica

I

The white snowflake fell,
landing with a thud. June: Damned
thing still not melted.

II

Limned in moonlight,
peach boughs wave. I don't wave back.
They give me heartburn.

III

A breeze sways the rose.
The butterfly resting there
is still. Drunk again?

IV

Aged willows bend,
whisper to the eager stream
warnings of oil slicks.

V

The mountain in spring
wears flowers; in cold, ermine.
Ostentatious fop.

VI

A gold harvest moon;
blue plums on a clean white plate.
I hanker for prunes.

COGNATE OBJECT

IV. Cognate Object— When a verb is followed by an object formed from the same root as the verb it is known as a Cognate Object. The old rhyme supplies a number of Cognate Objects:

So forth to steal he softly stole,
The bags of chink he chunk,
And many a wicked smile he smole
And many a wink he wunk.

(from a book on grammar)

Many a dope the crook did dupe
And slyful slink he slunk
Many a pupil he did pupe
And whyful think he thunk.

Many a fool the fellow felled
And darkful deed he done
Many the tall tale that he telled
And many the grin he grun.

He lived his life by cunning
And pocketed the poke
He thought of the sin he was sunning
And a smugful smirk he smoke.

One day he got salvationed
The Lord's Good Book he clutched
And now his soul's elevationed
For many the preach he prutched.

He went many a place he had wunt
Saw many a thief who thove
And said, 'Repent if you've not repunt,
Repent of the crime you crove.'

They thought of ruses he had rigged
And good luck he had lucked
So giggleful giggles they then gigged
And chuckleful chuckles chucked.

Many a grunt they grunted
Many a nod they node
For he left no stint unstunted
So many a cheer they chode.

'A rogue,' said one, 'can't mend his ways,
Phew! to his feckless feint;
Once a rogue, a rogue he stays
'Tis certain a saint he ain't!

'Twelvéty-times-eleven
Were the stealths he stealthéd, mates.
If he's set his sights on heaven,
It's to steal the pearly gates.'

Then many a rueful booh they booh'd,
Many a tongue-cluck clicked,
Many an Oohful Ooh they Ooh'd
And snickerful snicker snicked.

Many a gleeful glance they glunce
Many the tune did hum,
Many the fanciful dance they dunce
And many the rhyme they rhum.

OH DEAR,
THE THIRD NASTY THOUGHT OF
THE DAY, AND IT ISN'T EVEN
LUNCH TIME YET

Comparisons are odious, I thought,
Futile, tasteless, tedious and wearing.
Now I think they probably are not,
Compared with who or what one is comparing.

NOTES

The author acknowledges with sincere appreciation the invaluable assistance of Mr 'Abdu'lláh Miṣbáh and Dr Vaḥíd Ra'fatí in preparing and checking these notes.

JACKET DESIGN
Pebbles, by Audrey Marcus. Mrs Marcus, an American-born painter, a Bahá'í, has lived in Africa and Europe, and now makes her home in the Middle East. Her paintings, acclaimed by critics for their 'intimations of spirituality' and 'fresh and universal perceptivity' have been shown frequently in European galleries. Her work has been acquired by the Israel Museum and the National Museum of Luxembourg.

DEDICATION
The quotation is taken from *Prayers and Meditations by Bahá'u'lláh*, p. 144 (U.S. ed.), p. 110 (U.K. ed.).

PART ONE:
THE TRUE BROTHER
See the Will and Testament of 'Abdu'l-Bahá, p. 3, 25.

THE HELPMATE
The quotation is from Shoghi Effendi's letter to the National Spiritual Assembly of the Bahá'ís of Canada, printed without date in *Messages to Canada*: 'It was a member of that same community who won the immortal distinction of being called upon to be my helpmate, my shield in warding off the darts of Covenant-breakers and my tireless collaborator in the arduous tasks I shoulder.' 'Amatu'l-Bahá Rúḥíyyih Khánum has graciously consented to the publication of this poem but joins the author in the fervent hope that the reader will recognize the use of poetic licence in some of the images.

A WHISPERED EPITAPH
The Hand of the Cause John E. Esslemont, the 'Scottish disciple of 'Abdu'l-Bahá' is buried on Mt Carmel. The opening lines of the last stanza take cognizance of Samuel Johnson's statement: 'In

lapidary inscriptions a man is not upon oath.' Dr Esslemont's gravestone is inscribed: 'By all who knew him he was loved.' He is the distinguished author of *Bahá'u'lláh and the New Era*.

GEORGE TOWNSHEND

The opening quotation is given by Shoghi Effendi in *The Promised Day is Come*, pp. 105–15. George Townshend was in 1906 ordained a priest of the Protestant Episcopal Church in the United States and in 1933 was elected a Canon of St Patrick's Cathedral, Dublin. In that same year he also became Archdeacon of Clonfert. He encountered the Faith of Bahá'u'lláh in 1916 and was the recipient of two Tablets from 'Abdu'l-Bahá, one of which expressed the hope that he would bring his Church 'under the heavenly Jerusalem.' Throughout the years he wrote copiously for the Cause and in 1947 renounced his Orders in order to devote full time to the Bahá'í Faith— in Shoghi Effendi's words, 'a truly remarkable and historic step,' a deed 'that history will record and for which future generations will be deeply grateful and will extol and admire.'

George Townshend was appointed a Hand of the Cause in December 1951. At the invitation of Shoghi Effendi he wrote Introductions to *The Dawn-Breakers* and *God Passes By* and gave the books their titles. The incident that suggested the poem is one related by David Hofman in his forthcoming biography. A brief account of Mr Townshend's life appears in *The Bahá'í World*, vol. XIII, pp. 841–6.

OLYMPIC CHAMPION

Agnes Baldwin Alexander heard of the Bahá'í Faith in 1900 in Rome through Mrs Charlotte Dixon and was confirmed in it by May Ellis Bolles (Maxwell) in Paris shortly thereafter. She carried the Faith to her home in Hawaii, and later to Japan and Korea. Miss Alexander was elevated to the rank of Hand of the Cause in 1957. She is mentioned by name in 'Abdu'l-Bahá's *Tablets of the Divine Plan*. See also 'In Memoriam', *The Bahá'í World*, vol. XV. The poem is based on an incident described to me by Craig Quick of Hawaii. Some will remember the late Helen Hokinson's cartoons which delighted readers of *The New Yorker*.

The murder of the Hand of the Cause Enoch Olinga, his wife Elizabeth, and three of their children—Badí', Lennie and Ṭáhirih—was reported on 17 September 1979. Reference is made in the poem to the Kampala International Conference, one of six held in October 1967 to mark the centenary of Bahá'u'lláh's proclamation to the kings and rulers. The Kampala gathering was attended by approximately 500 Bahá'ís from 24 nations and is reported in *The Bahá'í World*, vol. XIV, p. 221. In October 1953 Enoch Olinga was named a Knight of Bahá'u'lláh for his service in introducing the Bahá'í Faith to the Cameroons, and in October 1957 he was named a Hand of the Cause. Shoghi Effendi bestowed upon him the title 'Father of Victories'. Mr Olinga was born in 1927 in Uganda and became a Bahá'í in 1952.

DANCING-MASTER

Raḥmatu'lláh Muhájir, with his wife, Írán, opened the Mentawai Islands to the Faith of Bahá'u'lláh for which service they were named Knights of Bahá'u'lláh. Dr Muhájir whose indefatigable world travels endeared him to the entire Bahá'í world was named a Hand of the Cause in October 1957. He died in December 1979. In various places throughout the Bahá'í Writings the Faith of Bahá'u'lláh is likened to music, the believers to dancers.

HISTORY LESSON

The opening quotation is from *Selections from the Writings of the Báb*, p. 124. Ḥasan M. Balyuzi was born in S͟híráz in a family distinguished for its scholarship and administrative ability. In 1939 he joined the Persian service of the British Broadcasting Corporation. He was a member of the National Spiritual Assembly of the Bahá'ís of the British Isles for many years and was appointed a Hand of the Cause in 1957. He is the author of a number of scholarly works related to the Bahá'í Faith including biographies of the three Central Figures of the Faith, his crowning work being his monumental Life of Bahá'u'lláh, the first volume of which has been published, and the second being now in preparation. He also wrote a Life of Muḥammad, *Muḥammad and the Course of Islám* (George Ronald, Oxford.)

Dr Adelbert Mühlschlegel, a physician, served on the National Spiritual Assembly of the Bahá'ís of Germany for many years and was appointed a Hand of the Cause in February 1952. He died in July 1980. In 1977 the Bahá'ís of Germany, to coincide with Dr Mühlschlegel's eightieth birthday, published a book of his poems, *Gedichte*, through *Bahá'í Verlag*, the German Publishing Trust.

IN MEMORIAM: A. Q. FAIZI

The opening quotation is from a cable of condolence sent by the Hand of the Cause William Sears on 21 November 1980. Mr Faizi was appointed a Hand of the Cause in October 1957. All who knew him remarked upon his extraordinary capacity to shower love upon everyone he met.

LINES FOR A WOMAN OF YAZD

'Alí-Aṣghar Shahíd was born in 1867/8 and, together with his 22 year old brother, was martyred in 1890/1 by an angry mob who carried the head of 'Alí-Aṣghar and threw it into a room in which his mother and his young bride were sitting. In a Tablet of the Master, as yet untranslated and published in English, He praises the mother for her action in cleansing the head and setting it outside the door, admonishing: 'What we have sacrificed in the path of God no man has the right to return to us.' An account of the event is found in Málmírí's *History of the Martyrs of Yazd*, a work as yet untranslated from the Persian. In oral transmission the story of this martyr is often confused with that of Siyyid Ashraf (see Shoghi Effendi, *God Passes By*, p. 199).

HEAVEN'S FOOL

The father of the young martyr Badí', Hájí 'Abdu'l-Majíd of Níshápúr, (now known as Níshábúr), a merchant of note, enlisted under the banner of Mullá Ḥusayn. He was the first to respond to his leader's request to leave behind all belongings by casting aside his satchel which contained his most treasured possession, a considerable amount of turquoise which had been brought with him from the mine that belonged to his father. See Nabíl-i-A'ẓam, *The Dawn-Breakers*, p. 329, and Shoghi Effendi, *God Passes By*, p. 39.

The opening words of 'Abdu'l-Bahá are found in *Memorials of the Faithful*, pp. 104–5.

THE COMFORTER

Myrta Perkins Swingle (later 'Sandoz') recorded her reminiscences which were compiled by her daughters, Eva Mae Barrow and Mildred Swingle Bates. The addresses 'Abdu'l-Bahá gave at the Swingle Sanitarium on 6 May 1912 are to be found in *The Promulgation of Universal Peace*, pp. 97–100; the photograph taken of a group at the Sanitarium appears in *Star of the West*, vol. III, no. 6, p. 5. Permission was obtained from Eva Mae Barrow to publish this poem which she said describes an event 'I almost failed to mention, fearing that my mother's seeming boldness would be misunderstood and not seen as the high-spirited action of a devoted and pure-hearted young girl.' The title of the poem was suggested by 'Abdu'l-Bahá's comment recorded in the pilgrim notes of Alice Mary Buckton of London. The Master asked, *'Do you not say in the West that this is the Day of the Comforter? Are you comforting? Are you doing the work of the Comforter?'* See *Star of the West*, vol. II, no. 1, p. 7.

IN MEMORIAM: MARGERY MCCORMICK

Beth McKenty's tribute to this outstanding Bahá'í teacher is found in *The Bahá'í World*, vol. XIV, pp. 362–4. The poem was suggested by a conversation its author had in which Mrs McCormick said she found it useful to cast both praise and blame over her shoulder into 'the Most Great Ocean' to avoid having her ego become inflated or her spirit saddened. Her earliest Bahá'í talks were given in Wilmette, sometimes to an audience of one—her chairman, Horace Holley.

REGINALD TURVEY

The poem was suggested by Lowell Johnson's memoir; see *The Bahá'í World*, vol. XIV, p. 385. Reginald Turvey became a Bahá'í in 1936 through Mark Tobey whom he met at Dartington Hall. Bernard Leach, Mark Tobey and Reginald Turvey became lifelong friends. Shoghi Effendi referred to Turvey as 'the spiritual father of South Africa.' Increasingly Turvey's paintings are being acclaimed for their 'spiritual perception.'

THE GIFT

See 'In Memoriam', *The Bahá'í World*, vol. XV, pp. 468–73.

DISTINCTION

The statement attributed to Curtis DeMude Kelsey is from his 'In Memoriam', see reference above. The quotation from 'Abdu'l-Bahá is found in May Maxwell's *An Early Pilgrimage*, p. 42.

INDIAN SUMMER

See 'In Memoriam', *The Bahá'í World*, vol. XVI, p. 514; *'Abdu'l-Bahá* by H. M. Balyuzi, p. 265; 'Teaching the Canadian Indians', (in) *Messages [of Shoghi Effendi] to Canada*, pp. 16, 73. Those familiar with the work of the noted Canadian poet Wilfred Campbell (1858–1918) will recognize the salute to his poem 'Indian Summer' published in 1889.

RECOGNITION

Allan Raynor is a distinguished Canadian Bahá'í who served for many years on the National Spiritual Assembly of Canada. The poem was suggested by conversations its author had with Mr Raynor during his final pilgrimage to the Holy Land shortly before his death in September 1979 in his sixty-eighth year.

PAUSING

The American poet Robert Hayden was born in 1913 in Detroit, Michigan. In 1966, comments Mr Breman in tribute to Mr Hayden, 'his *A Ballad of Remembrance* found belated recognition and justification when it won Hayden, through tireless promotion by Rosey Pool and Langston Hughes, the Grand Prix de la Poésie of the Dakar First World Festival of Negro Arts.' Mr Hayden served for two years as consultant in poetry to the Library of Congress and was a professor of English at the University of Michigan. In 1971 he was awarded the Russel Loines Award for poetry by the National Institute of Arts and Letters and in 1975 received an award from the Academy of American Poets. His works of poetry include: *American Journal, Angle of Ascent, The Night-Blooming Cereus, Words in the Mourning Time, Kaleidoscope, Heart-Shape in the Dust, Figure of Time* and *A Ballad of Remembrance.*

A PLACE BEYOND

The persona of the poem is fictitious. The 'prayer' with which the poem concludes is not part of the Bahá'í Writings, but is the composition of the author of the poem.

THE INDISCRETION OF MARIE-THÉRÈSE BEAUCHAMPS

The character and incident are fictitious. The year 1962 marked the fiftieth anniversary of the visit of 'Abdu'l-Bahá to Montreal, Canada—a sojourn extending from 30 August to 9 September 1912. For the first few days He was the guest of Mr and Mrs William Sutherland Maxwell at their home on Pine Avenue West on Mount Royal, a building now designated a Bahá'í Shrine; and later He moved to a suite at the Windsor Hotel when the press of guests grew so great that He feared inconveniencing His hosts. The *Gazette* and *Montreal Daily Star* of that period gave generous coverage to 'Abdu'l-Bahá's addresses. Of His visit, 'Abdu'l-Bahá said: *'The time of the sojourn was limited to a number of days, but the results in the future are inexhaustible.'*

The author is grateful to Michael Power for his translation of this piece into what I am assured is the 'French of Montreal spoken in the period.'

L'année 1962 a marqué le cinquantième anniversaire de la visite d' 'Abdu'l-Bahá à Montréal où Il est resté du 30 août au 9 septembre 1912. Au début de son séjour, Il était l'invité de M. et Mme Sutherland Maxwell. (Leur maison, située sur l'avenue des pins ouest à Mont Royal, est maintenant un sanctuaire bahá'í.) Mais quelques jours plus tard, lorsque les visiteurs devinrent trop nombreux, Il craignit que ses hôtes fussent incommodés et Il prit alors une suite à l'Hôtel Windsor. Le *Gazette* et le *Montreal Daily Star* de l'époque parlèrent amplement des discours d' 'Abdu'l-Bahá. En parlant de Sa visite, 'Abdu'l-Bahá a dit: 'Le temps du séjour n'a été que de quelques jours mais les résultats dans l'avenir seront sans fin.'

La narratrice ainsi que l'événement décrits dans cette nouvelle sont fictifs.

SOME SORT OF FOREIGNER

The incident upon which this piece is based is related by Lady Blomfield in *The Chosen Highway*, p. 152; the epigraph is taken from the same book, p. 175.

CRIMINAL MAESTRO

Barbara Barrett's translation is of the poem 'Master Criminal' which appears on p. 8 of *Another Song, Another Season*. The story of Eduardo Duarte Vieira is found in his 'In Memoriam', *The Bahá'í World*, vol. XIV, pp. 389–90. The poem was suggested by the words of Bahá'u'lláh in *Prayers and Meditations by Bahá'u'lláh* in which, referring to the faithful, He says *'Thou knowest full well, O my God, that their only crime is to have loved Thee.'*

PART TWO:

SONG FOR A SORCERER

The opening quotation is from 'Abdu'l-Bahá, *The Promulgation of Universal Peace*, (Chicago, 1922), vol. II, p. 431, and is from a discourse delivered in New York.

TRYST

The opening quotation is from *Gleanings from the Writings of Bahá'u'-lláh*, XLII. This theme of fidelity and commitment also draws upon *The Hidden Words*, stanzas 8, 15, 19 and 23 from the Arabic; stanzas 1, 4, 14, 22, 31 and 77 from the Persian. Bahá'u'lláh's use of hyacinths as a symbol of divine knowledge is here deliberately reversed to represent secular wisdom.

THE SONG OF KHADÍJIH-BAGUM

Some readers will recognize the salute to the early poem by E. E. Cummings, 'All in Green Went My Love Riding'. The quotation attributed to H. M. Balyuzi is from his dedication to his *Life of the Báb*; the fragment from the *Qayyúmu'l-Asmá'*, in Mr Balyuzi's translation, appears on p. 47 of that work.

CRIMES

The poem was suggested by Bahá'u'lláh's statement in *Prayers and Meditations by Bahá'u'lláh*, (p. 23 US ed., p. 16 UK ed.), *'Thou knowest full well, O my God, that their only crime is to have loved Thee . . .'* (referring to the oppressed Bahá'ís.)

THE JOURNEY

The passage from the Qur'án is cited by Bahá'u'lláh in *The Seven Valleys and the Four Valleys*, (p. 45 US ed.) See also 'Abdu'l-Bahá, *Selections from the Writings of 'Abdu'l-Bahá*, p. 240: *'. . . in loving Him, at every moment there are hardships, torments, afflictions.'*

ṬÁHIRIH'S SONG

I am indebted to Mr 'Abdu'lláh Miṣbah for the information upon which this note is based. *Váv*, the character in the Persian alphabet representing 'v', and the character' (*Alif*), are symbols of the Manifestation of God in eastern mystical literature. The character '(*'Ayn*) is charged with poetic significance; its meanings include 'source' and 'eye'. The Mystery of the Great Reversal spoken of by Shaykh-Aḥmad-i-Aḥsá'í, one of the 'twin resplendent lights' who heralded the Báb and Bahá'u'lláh, was alluded to by Bahá'u'lláh in His *Kitáb-i-Aqdas*, and plays upon the numerical significance of the letters 'v' (6) and 'a' (1), *Váv*. In *God Passes By*, p. 54, Shoghi Effendi describes the Báb as 'standing at the confluence of two universal prophetic cycles, the Adamic Cycle stretching back as far as the first dawnings of the world's recorded religious history, and the Bahá'í Cycle destined to propel itself across the unborn reaches of time for a period of no less than five thousand centuries.' Thus the Báb, represented by the figure one, stands between the Adamic Cycle (6) and the Revelation of Bahá'u'lláh (6), the latter being equivalent in power to the total of all previous religious dispensations. Another meaning of 'reversal' referred to in the Bahá'í Writings is that of the debased being exalted, the mighty brought low, etc., with the coming of a new Revelation, a theme frequently developed by 'Abdu'l-Bahá throughout His addresses. *Bahjí* literally means 'delight' but also refers to that part of the plain of 'Akká where the Shrine and Mansion of Bahá'u'lláh are located.

IN LIEU OF PANEGYRIC

The quotation from Shoghi Effendi is found on p. 400 of *God Passes By*. Other heroines mentioned in this passage are Keith Ransom-Kehler, Susan Moody and Lillian Kappes.

INK

The sonnet was suggested by stanza 71 (Arabic) of *The Hidden Words*: '*O Son of Man! Write all that We have revealed unto thee with the ink of light upon the tablet of thy spirit. Should this not be in thy power, then make thine ink of the essence of thy heart . . .*'
'Lees'— at banquets in ancient Greece a lover might tip out from the cup the dregs of the wine and with the finger write the name of the loved one.

SILENCES

The poem grew out of a conversation about the literary silences of many who were great in achievement— Hardy, Melville, Rimbaud, Gerard Manley Hopkins— not the 'natural' silences, necessary for renewal of the creative process, but the unnatural thwarting of what struggles to come into being.

DREAM SONG

The verse alludes to a number of personages, events and passages from Bahá'í Writings. The central theme is 'the Mystery of the Great Reversal'— see note for *Ṭáhirih's Song* given above. Individuals specifically referred to are Nabíl (shepherd), Ṭáhirih (bell, bride), Ḥají Sulaymán Khán (candelabrum). Bahá'u'lláh wrote in His *Súriy-i-Ra'ís* of the future of Adrianople (the Land of Mystery) '. . . *the trees on the mountain will weep.*' The lover burning in the sea echoes a Persian mystical poem cited by Bahá'u'lláh in *The Seven Valleys*. One feasting on his heart alludes to a prayer by Bahá'u'lláh:

'. . . the food of them who haste to meet Thee is the fragments of their broken hearts.' Sun rising in the west: see 'America and the Most Great Peace' in *The World Order of Bahá'u'lláh*, by Shoghi Effendi, p. 75.

CHOICES

The opening quotation is from the address of the Hand of the Cause William Sears to the International Bahá'í Convention, Haifa, 1978, and was recorded stenographically by the author of the poem.

AN IRISH AIR

The poem recognizes indebtedness to the Hand of the Cause George Townshend who, at Shoghi Effendi's invitation, gave *God Passes By* its title, and pays tribute to two lines from Yeats's poem 'September 1913': 'You'd cry: Some woman's yellow hair/Has maddened every mother's son.'

CAPRICCIO

See 'Abdu'l-Bahá, *Selections from the Writings of 'Abdu'l-Bahá*, p. 256: '. . . In this, the Bahá'í dispensation, God's Cause is spirit unalloyed . . . its one crusade is against the insistent self, the evil promptings of the human heart.'

GROOM'S SONG

The poem is not based upon an historical incident but draws upon recorded statements from which it may be inferred that the Báb was an expert horseman. See Nabíl-i-A'ẓam, *The Dawn-Breakers*, pp. 148, 209, 309. The opening quotation is from the same source, p. 260.

CORAL AND PEARLS

The opening quotation is drawn from two prayers for marriage, one appearing in *Selections from the Writings of 'Abdu'l-Bahá*, p. 119, and the other in Bahá'í Prayers (pp. 187–188, US ed.) The phrase beginning 'He hath let loose the two seas . . .' is from the Qur'án 55:19–22.

PART THREE:

Shoghi Effendi's words, on the divider page, are found in *God Passes By*, p. 277.

SONG FOR THE WAITING STONES

The poem was suggested by the words of Bahá'u'lláh cited by Shoghi Effendi in 'The Dispensation of Bahá'u'lláh' (*World Order of Bahá'u'lláh*, p. 106): '*North and South both vibrate to the call announcing the advent of our Revelation. We can hear the voice of Mecca acclaiming: 'All praise be to Thee, O Lord my God, the All-Glorious, for having wafted over me the breath redolent with the fragrance of Thy presence!' Jerusalem, likewise, is calling aloud: 'Lauded and magnified art Thou, O Beloved of earth and heaven, for having turned the agony of my separation from Thee into the joy of a life-giving reunion!'*

THOUGHTS ON BLINDNESS

'Crimson Ark'—see *Gleanings from the Writings of Bahá'u'lláh* LXXXVI; 'Voice of the Crier' (The Báb) and 'The Ruler' (Bahá'u'lláh) see *Tablets of Bahá'u'lláh revealed after the Kitáb-i-Aqdas*, pp. 9–17.

PRAYER FOR THE TRUE BELIEVER

Mary of Magdala is spoken of in the highest terms in the Writings of the Bahá'í Faith; 'Abdu'l-Bahá is recorded in the unpublished diary of Juliet Thompson as saying that the mention of the Magdalen's name never failed to bring a smile of happiness to the face of Bahá'u'lláh. She is often alluded to as a symbol of the 'true believer'. In *Gleanings from the Writings of Bahá'u'lláh* LXXIII it is stated that the '*existence and life*' of '*the true believer*' are '*to be regarded as the originating purpose of all creation.*'

SIGHTSEEING

A visit to the graveyard in 'Akká is not part of the programme of pilgrimage to the Holy Land for Bahá'ís. On this occasion the author was accompanying Bahá'ís who had obtained permission to offer prayers at the resting place of members of their family.

THE VISITORS

The opening quotation referring to pilgrims is found in *Selections from the Writings of 'Abdu'l-Bahá*, pp. 195–6.

THE TROUBLE WITH MOUNTAINS

Bahá'u'lláh describes Himself as having feet of steel (see *The Promised Day is Come*, p. 85); and bids His followers to advance with *'sharp sight . . . adamant soul . . . on brass-like feet'* (see *Gleanings from the Writings of Bahá'u'lláh* CXV).

THE DYNAMICS OF EDEN

The opening quotation is found in *Bahá'í World Faith*, p. 330.

THE REPLENISHMENT OF WONDER

The commemoration of the Ascension of Bahá'u'lláh is observed in the Holy Land in the Ḥaram-i-Aqdas, Bahjí, at 1:45 a.m. on May 29th. The room in which Bahá'u'lláh passed away in the Mansion is open and here one may offer prayers. Beside His bed are His slippers, heaped with rose petals. This provides the theme of the poem. In this room Bahá'u'lláh received Professor E. G. Browne, one of the few Westerners to have met Him.

EDEN, AND ALL THAT

'Abdu'l-Bahá, in *The Promulgation of Universal Peace*, states that *'when women participate fully and equally in the affairs of the world . . . war will cease; for women will be the obstacle and hindrance to it. This is true and without doubt.'* And again, *'The education of woman will be a mighty step towards [war's] abolition . . . for she will use her whole influence against war . . . she will refuse to give her sons for sacrifice upon the field of battle. In truth she will be the greatest factor in establishing universal peace and international arbitration.'*

DRILL

Bahá'u'lláh in the *Kitáb-i-Íqán* (pp. 8–9 US ed., p. 6 UK ed.) cites the quotation which heads the poem. For an instance of the Báb doing so see Nabíl-i-A'ẓam, *The Dawn-Breakers*, p. 311.

'Litotes' is defined by the poet, Frances Stillman, as 'a whimsical kind of understatement which affirms something by denying its opposite.' Litotes, as the author's recollection of his early years with his Sligo-born grandmother confirms, appears frequently in the speech patterns of the Irish. The poem is an almost verbatim record of the reply.

LINES FOR A NEW BELIEVER

Bahá'u'lláh frequently likens His Revelation to an ocean into which those who truly believe in Him must cast themselves. Most attracted are the 'pure in heart'— traditionally symbolized by children. The saints 'drown' themselves in the love of God.

PART FOUR:

CONFRONTATION

The poem is rooted in 'The Daimonic in Dialogue', chapter 6 of Rollo May's *Love and Will*.

YOUNG MAN, OLD MAN

The opening line is a surviving fragment of a poem by an anonymous author.

MARK'S MADRIGAL

The quotation is taken from Marzieh Gail's 'The Days with Mark Tobey', *World Order* magazine, Spring 1977.

SPENDTHRIFT

Some scholars hold that this question 'Am I not your Lord?' is put to every human soul as it comes into being.

LEDA'S SONG

Some will recognize that the author follows the mystical tradition in employing Leda as a symbol of the human condition. See also Lilian Bowes Lyon's 'Leda'.

An excellent discussion of psychic death can be found in Abraham H. Maslow's *Toward a Psychology of Being*.

FIGURES IN A GARDEN

The opening quotation is from 'Words of Wisdom', *Tablets of Bahá'u'lláh revealed after the Kitáb-i-Aqdas*, p. 156. The quotation from *Bahá'u'lláh and the New Era* is from p. 18 of the 1970 American edition.

Ṭáhirih, 'The Pure One', was born in Qazvín, Persia. She is the only woman among the Letters of the Living, and the first woman suffrage martyr. She went to her death anointed with perfume and clad as a bride. She was strangled with a silk scarf in a garden in Ṭihrán and her body lowered into a well which was then filled with earth and stones.

As early as 1853, when she was only 23 years old, Emily Dickinson remarked in a letter to a friend, 'I do not go from home.' By the time she was 30 she had become an almost total recluse in her father's home. Having rejected the traditional Puritan conception of God and withdrawn from her church in her mid-twenties, she followed her own spiritual path. Immortality, a dominant theme in her poetry and letters, she called 'the flood subject.' Her voluntary hermitage, one who knew her has written, 'was not due to any love-disappointment, nor was she an invalid. She had tried society and the world and found them lacking.'

PART FIVE:

'Abdu'l-Bahá's words, on the divider page, are found in *Selections from the Writings of 'Abdu'l-Bahá*, p. 24.

PICNIC AT THE HILTON

The incident which suggested the piece is found in Elena Maria Marsella's memoir of the Hand of the Cause Agnes Baldwin Alexander, *The Bahá'í World*, vol. XV, pp. 423–30.

An illuminating description of the role of fear and anxiety in block-
ing off authentic religious experience is found in *Your Emotional
Conflicts* by Peter Fletcher, Pan Books, 1958, 1963.

MINOR ARTIST

Dotan Uziel is a well-known Israeli child artist whose remarkable
drawings have been compared by critics to Picasso's. The incident
described in the poem occurred during a television interview in
1979.

UNFINISHED BUSINESS

Carole Lombard Gable attended Bahá'í classes as a child and at age 14
wrote to 'Abdu'l-Bahá expressing her love for Him and her ambi-
tions and longings, in response to which she received His Tablet
praying for her success. Her acceptance of the Bahá'í Faith in her
adult years is recorded in the April 1938 issue of the Los Angeles
Bahá'í Newsletter. She died in a plane crash on 16 January 1942. Her
'In Memoriam' appears in *The Bahá'í World,* vol. IX, pp. 635–7.
The concluding quotations are from *Selections from the Writings of
'Abdu'l-Bahá*, pages 204, 246.

PART SIX:

FOR MEN ONLY

Phonaesthesia is defined by Simeon Potter as 'sound-meaning associa-
tions which would seem to be not merely echoic or onomatopoeic
but rather linguistically innate and universal.'

'IF YOU'RE GOING TO TALK WATERMELON, PRISSY . . .'

In David O. Selznick's 1939 epic *Gone With the Wind*, Prissy was
played by Butterfly McQueen who is now employed as a play-
ground assistant in Harlem (see *Time*, 26 January 1981, under
'People'.)

PART SEVEN:

OF STATES AND STATESMEN

Julius Caesar, Act I, sc. ii, line 18.

SPORTS

Bobby Hull, the internationally acclaimed hockey star, spent his childhood in Belleville, Ontario and befriended the author's family.